The Men Out There

The Men Out There

A Woman's Little Black Book

by Susan R. Shapiro and Michele Kasson, Ph.D.

Rutledge Books, Inc.   Bethel, CT

Copyright © 1997 by Susan R. Shapiro and Michele Kasson, Ph.D.

ALL RIGHTS RESERVED
Rutledge Books, Inc.
8 F.J. Clarke Circle, Bethel, CT 06801

Manufactured in the United States of America

Cataloging in Publication Data
Shapiro, Susan R. (Susan Ripps)
   The men out there : a woman's little black book /
by Susan R. Shapiro and Michele Kasson.
     p. cm.
   ISBN 1-887750-37-1
   1. Mate selection--United States. 2. Man-woman relationships. 3. Men--United States--Psychology. 4. Single women--United States--Psychology. I. Kasson, Michele. II. Title.
646.77--dc20   LC 96-71015
                                                         CIP

For our children

Man never falls so low that he can see nothing higher than himself.

—Theodore Parker

For men at most differ as heaven and earth.

—Idylls of the Kin, Merlin and Vivien

ACKNOWLEDGEMENTS

We are indebted to many people. Gary Barash and Ross Graison deserve a special mention for the time, patience and care they have given us. Gary, in particular, for his vast repertoire of quotations. Ross, in particular, for his unrelenting moral support.

Both of our families have been steadfast through our vigil. Our close friends have contributed their energy and thoughts. Keith Korman foresaw the potential of our notion and guided us. The team at Rutledge Books; Ken Karlan, Meryl Moss, Alison Karl, and Nina Otero have understood our vision from day one. It is their insight that has brought this book to life. Richard Belson and Donald Cohen, our initial audiences, were capable and wise. Michele Davis, Harriet Goldman, Jay Gould, and Michael Mantz were sounding boards for certain concepts. Angela Marius kept peace at home and Antoinette Michaels faxed relevant material.

The unnamed women who have come forward to share their tales have made this book possible. In the interest of privacy, identifying characteristics have been changed. Their personal accounts are earnest and intriguing. The men out there need to be thanked as well—without them the lives of these women would be unidimensional.

Our children, Michael Kasson-Loebl, Jennie Shapiro Ripps, Michael Shapiro Ripps and Elizabeth Shapiro Ripps, each merit our deepest gratitude. Their love and devotion is felt at every moment. They are our champions.

CONTENTS

The Men Out There 1

PART I
The Seducer/Immediate Relationships

1 The Narcissist/Disarmer
   Men who make you feel good 11

2 Ambivalence Syndrome
   He's unpredictable and impatient.
   You need to be steadfast 27

3 Instant Family Man and Widowers
   Ideal for divorced women with children..........47

4 Commitment Phobic and Serially Monogamous
   You could be the winner 62

5 The Addict
   Show him the way 79

PART II
The Lost Boys

6 Money and Power
   Learn to live with his toys 99

7 Champion Sport/Macho Man
   Aggressive and fearless. Improve your
   swing 121

8 The Workaholic, Sexaholic and Gambling Man
   Anesthetizers and escape artists 139

PART III
Sex and Love

9 The Stoic/Woman as Objet d'Art
   Emotionless, routine sex.
      Teach him to feel 157

10 The Married Man
   Hope against hope 174

11 Sex/The Connection
   The key to intimacy 194

12 The Man I Love
   The difference is obvious 209

Afterword:
   The lessons learned about the
      men out there 225

The Men Out There

One enters the world of being single with great trepidation and uncertainty. For the multitude of women who are divorced with or without children, there is little knowledge of what awaits them once they muster the courage to leave a long standing marriage. More often than not, serious emotional damage is the residue of the marriage. Once the healing begins and single status becomes a reality, the questions persist, is there a man out there who is worthy? Is he gentle, moral, kind, and fairly problem free? While women and men become single or remain single at any age and stage of their lives, the predominant population of single women and men appear to range in mid-age, from thirty-five to fifty-five. Single women in mid-age vary in their needs, but a common thread is their desire to be reunited with a mate. Their hope prevails, despite their experiences with the men out there.

Women need a means to recognize the variety of men and personality styles. Without this recognition the entire search for a mate is bewildering. Where do these men come from and what has occurred in their lives or their marriages? Have we as middle aged women, truly given up the dream of a knight in shining armor? Are our expectations too great and our damage too severe? Is there such a rare creature as the compassionate, thoughtful man? Are we even equipped to handle him, to recognize him?

The Men Out There offers single women in mid-age insight into what to expect and how to handle these men. After reading the innermost secrets of women who have dated and been in relationships, the reader will have a keen sense of how to best obtain a successful relationship in their own lives. Our intention is to educate women to recognize common patterns. To achieve this goal each chapter focuses on only one aspect of character or behavior, but this does not negate the richness of personality in us all. Therefore, our book will walk any and every woman through a variety of experiences, so that we become better educated.

There are many kinds of relationships, and each is unique. However, there are certain scenarios which are played out time and again. The common theme becomes apparent. As the reader, one will recognize herself in these stories and hopefully learn how to prevent future mishaps, and to be self protected. Our book offers the opportunity to take in the trials and tribulations of relationships. By the time you have completed reading *The Men Out There*, your chances of getting it right will be greatly enhanced.

With this in mind, we enter the arena, meeting men any place; at work, at parties, through friends, at bars, restaurants, airports, at train stations. The stranger we meet may be anyone from a Federal Express delivery man to a brain surgeon. He is, initially, polished, smart, appealing and available. He confides his story to you and if you are intrigued or comfortable you confide yours to him. The boundaries are porous because both of you have suffered, and are embarking on a new life. There is complete empathy as the scenario unfolds. The ex-wife was a witch, your ex-husband an ogre. Money, child support, these are the on-going issues. Often bitterness pervades even the finest specimen, but does not manifest immediately. You have a drink, you go to dinner, a movie. You believe that you have common goals and values. You call your friends and confide that you have found a prince. This time he's a winner, not like last month's mutant. If a woman is wise, she will research her newest date. Most often she relies on her own opinion, unbiased and fresh, which seems fair and reasonable.

Quickly the balance shifts; you find yourself waiting for his phone calls, no longer asking a friend if her cousin from Milwaukee who is freshly divorced will indeed be in town. It is not significant now, instead, you have found this potential partner. All your eggs are getting placed, despite your better instincts, into one basket. What we are likely to forget in this early, euphoric state, is how to listen, to hear what this man tells us. If you are able to listen, he will tell you everything you need to know. The evidence will speak for itself. Instead, we are too busy noticing how well he is aging, or that his eyes sparkle. He has, thankfully, a sense of humor. He is generous when you eat out, and orders up a storm. But what is he really saying about his ex-wife, his mother, his childhood, his children, his career, his ex-partner he now loathes with a vengeance. And what does it mean?

Through the confidences shared in our book, we are reminded that men and women are not alike, and do not trade in the same emotional currency. *Until women recognize what it is that they want they cannot seek a partner who will suit their needs.* Too many women are ready to give up their own needs for the sake of the trappings of the relationship. However, none of us can get what we want until we are ready to put what we have on the line. If a relationship is not giving us what we need we have to be ready to give it up rather than to disregard our own feelings. If not, we find that we lose ourselves, thus relinquishing all of the power in the relationship to the man. Once we are ready to give up an impaired liason, the balance of power shifts again. Despite this knowledge, we fail to understand who this man is. Are we truly still *in love with love*, as we were twenty-five years ago? Or are we ready to take a hard look at what we want and will or will not accept. Our book provides salvation. By reading it you can avoid any confusion that is generated by the men out there.

Ideally, we seek a partner who will elicit the best qualities in each of us and makes it possible for one to complement the other. But if a woman repeats her mistakes and does not break the negative pattern, only initially will the relationship feel good. Ultimately, the man she has chosen becomes her partner in a hellish doom of repeating her own past.

The dating game continues; we are no wiser but older. Many of us have children who are small, others have adolescent children and others have grown children. We all know something about life, something about men. None of us is twenty-two. And yet as these men march toward us, we forget ourselves; our feminist leanings, our dashed hopes, our experiences, our joys. We focus on the man of the moment. But who is he? Not what your friends whisper, not how he reads on paper, not what his achievements are, his successes, his place in the community.

On paper, everyone looks good. At a party, every man is a winner. Standing in a crowded cocktail gathering, one man in particular sings to you. His eyes, smile, his body language, the texture of his suit, the colors in his tie. He has a mustache and you love mustaches. He wears a pony tail and you find this appealing. He confesses right off that he is an avid tennis player and so are you. You come from the same part of the country. Your are in the same field. In the beginning the illusion holds up and so the dance begins.

_____ Susan R. Shapiro and Michele Kasson, Ph.D.

The dance and desire of relationship at best, the fast spin of a few pleasant dates at worst.

It is a small wonder that so many of us are baffled. The men out there are complex; they come in all sizes, ages and attitudes with a full array of wishes and desires of their own. By mid-age there are, however, certain recurrent themes. These men are set in their ways and comfortable in their lifestyles. Our intention is to guide you in recognizing patterns of behavior that can either enhance or detract from any relationship. In reading this book you will learn how to achieve a profitable relationship. We have purposely not addressed the characteristics of women, but have chosen to explore the men that they pursue. While the path is arduous, and nuances are all pervasive, these men can be revealed.

There are certain men who believe that women are fungible, and can be interchanged indiscriminately. An example of this is a man who has had several wives. He has substituted one for the other. *It is not the structure of the marriage which changes, only the woman.* To this man, the particular woman doesn't matter. Until he meets you. You could be the one to change his life. Yet his track record is not great and it is your responsibility to increase your knowledge of his style in relationships. To have a heightened awareness is to be forewarned.

Numerous men have given up wives and lifestyles because their situation was unbearable. They suffer the repercussions especially when children are involved. They may be disenchanted with their careers, even if they have been a great success. They might feel as if they have achieved a tremendous amount but have sold out to the demands of wealth and status. Their lives are hollow at the core. These men in particular question their contribution to the world. The other side of the coin are the men who have believed in working toward higher goals and has not succeeded. This man feels as if he has missed out on the chance to be a success and to make it in the world. Both types of men have personal and career issues to deal with along with specific personality traits. By the time they have approached mid-life, these men are bewildered, ready for a woman to revolutionize their lives.

In reading this book you shall grow wiser, and each man you encounter will seem less formidable. Thousand upon thousands of women have lived what you are now living. You shall read their stories and recognize what is required to master a relationship and when to leave one that does not work. You will be better equipped to communicate with your partner and to understand his needs. Subsequently he will understand yours. With understanding and the ability to spot the trend, you can maximize the strengths, break the patterns and bad habits, and minimize the weaknesses. While none of us is perfect, the opportunity to enhance a relationship is now ours.

The opposite sexes spin their spins and the best behavior curtain is dropped. The second act begins, where the woman and the man share the mundane. The pieces of day to day living surface and one's perception is quickly altered. Whatever our mate does to cope in life is now apparent. If he is well balanced, there is a plurality of ways in which he deals with situations. If not, he may be set in a routine and only one style emerges. We have to ask ourselves if this man is incomplete, if he is, in fact, too damaged to be anything but bad news. If he falls into a rut, it is a signal to run the other way. The more he uses only one method of dealing with life, the more treacherous a situation. When we see the men out there who do not connect, there may not be a reason to stay and frantically patch it together. Each of us needs to learn what style of man can make us happy.

_____ Susan R. Shapiro and Michele Kasson, Ph.D.

In order to avoid making the same mistake twice, we recommend that a woman pay close attention to what she had before in a relationship, and to address why she was so unhappy with the situation. The chances are that in either a marriage or in a long term relationship, she may have been drawn to similar characteristics as the man she presently seeks as a partner. If she gains insight into this and determines that she desires change, she can then guide her path, and improve her life. She is presently in a position to make the right decision, to better her own life.

For example, a woman may be repeatedly drawn to a disarmer. He has won her heart through his charm and he has not let her near him. She knows less about this man now than on the first date. After many episodes of entering a room and spotting a handsome man who is the center of attention, she will know better than to be lured by him. She will no longer be smitten by his response. When she develops a rapport with this man she operates from power and is no longer blind to his demeanor. Her encounters have given her insight into what she will or will not tolerate in a mate. She is capable of a relationship with the man of her choice.

By reading these innermost tales of self-revelation, and working through the side bars, you will be better equipped to embrace a satisfying partnership. The types of men described in our book may be lacking in some ways, but are also fabulous, with numerous redeeming qualities. *Just as there is hope and flexibility in each of our journeys, there is potential in many relationships, and in the types of men which we uncover.* In recognizing our own feminine strengths and failings, can we learn to recognize the attributes of others. Now we are schooled and repaired, thus ready for the men out there. The eventuality is that the men become true possibilities and an entire universe is at our feet. The second half is about to begin.

Part I

The Seducer/ Immediate Relationships

1

*"So tell me who do I see when I look in your eyes?
Is that you baby, or just a brilliant disguise?"*
— Bruce Springsteen

THE NARCISSIST/DISARMER

The Greek myth of Narcissus was based on the story of a handsome hunter who broke the hearts of many women. Echo, who suffered at the hands of Narcissus, eventually wasted away from grief and longing for him until all that remained was her voice. Finally, one spurned female asked the goddess Hera to show Narcissus unrequited love. To this end, Hera led him to a pool where he fell in love with his own image. Consumed by self-adoration, he was unable to tear himself away from his reflection. There he pined away and died. All that remained was a white flower that we now call Narcissus.

Today we consider someone narcissistic if he has an unbalanced belief in himself, to the extent that he excludes the feelings of others. The narcissist represents someone who considers only himself. While the myth implies that narcissism is a negative quality, in fact, the intact personality is able to use narcissism to positive ends. *Narcissism is one aspect of character which can be employed for the attainment of happiness and satisfaction in daily life. A healthy narcissism entails a belief in oneself, the ability to recognize one's desires and needs, and to successfully obtain these goals.*

A healthy personality utilizes his narcissistic qualities to gain satisfaction in life. He remains capable of considering the thoughts, feelings and wishes of the people who surround him. However, as narcissism takes over as the *major* feature of someone's personality, these attributes which can work positively to enhance one's life then become negative. *In relationships with women, the narcissist will seek out a winner.* Because he needs other people to idolize him, the relationships he establishes are based on the admiration of others. The "winner" that the narcissist chooses is very specific to his requirements. Initially the chosen woman feels exceptionally good when she is with her narcissist. Her narcissist is pleased with her and shows her to the world.

At this juncture, the woman often sees the narcissist as a person who has it all. He has money, talent, wealth, looks and power, and a woman on his arm every step of the way. These men are envied by other men and by those who work with them. They prove to be quite successful in their careers and in their relationships. The relationships, however, are circumscribed. It is when his partner searches for more substance that the narcissist gets into trouble. In order for the woman in his life to succeed with him, she requires a deep understanding of his needs.

> **WHO HE CHOOSES**
> *Any woman who enhances him*
> *A young, beautiful trophy wife*
> *A high achiever, doctor or lawyer*
> *An obedient woman who idolizes him*

Susan R. Shapiro and Michele Kasson, Ph.D.

LESS REGARD FOR THE RIGHTS OF OTHERS

In a relationship with a narcissist/disarmer, a woman notes that he is warm in a one sided fashion. They discuss their interests, but his are more important. What is significant is how much of life is lived on his terms. The narcissist may be self-involved, thus unable to make an emotional commitment to another.

Within the sphere of narcissists, there are a variety of scenarios based on the depth and degree of the narcissism. The degree of narcissism is a determinant in the success of the relationship. Some result with great success, others do not. For instance, two years ago, when Alice, at thirty-eight, met Len, who was forty-four, he appeared to be handsome and gracious. He exuded the presence of a man who had everything, and had failed at nothing except his first marriage. He knew what he wanted and how to get it, in every realm. Alice was quite taken with him. As a litigator, Len experienced the admiration of an audience. He seemed to perform in all aspects of his life. His work gave him a position of leadership and authority. Everyone looked up to him and he had an excellent reputation.

"He did everything well and I was in awe, despite my own accomplishments. I was so smitten with him that I paid little attention to the tell tale signs. I didn't listen when he spoke of being the only son in a middle class family where he was considered the prince. His parents felt blessed to have had him. He was raised with this sense of entitlement. He never had the creative leaning of his two younger sisters, but he said that it affected him very little. He disparaged anything that wasn't a linear intelligence, but I think he felt this set him apart from his family."

Alice, as a creative director of an ad agency, offered Len his missing piece. To others, Len appeared to have it all, but beneath the facade, Len felt inadequate. Alice provided the credibility for Len that he felt was lacking in his relationships with his family.

"The lawyer jokes stopped because I was legitimately artistic. He calmed down and the first six months of the relationship were a whirlwind romance. I was on Len's arm for every firm function. After several months, I wanted to settle back into my own routine. I wanted to commit myself to the relationship and to my job. This superficial lifestyle was not for me. Len became more distant. Within a year I began to ask myself what I had done wrong.

"I was so frustrated when he would not face the issues. Our relationship headed for a downward spiral. I was no longer the princess. No matter what I did he was critical of me. I felt that I had to walk on eggshells when I was around him. He was aware of this too, and we spoke about it, but he had no insight into what brought on these feelings. I suspect that I stopped making him feel larger than life."

> **HE DOES NOT WISH TO REVEAL HIMSELF**
> *He seeks out the limelight*
> *His charm masks his emptyness*
> *Serious discussions may expose him*
> *He needs you there to enhance him*

Alice tormented herself with questions. "I felt very responsible for the failing relationship, and I became depressed. I wondered how I had changed. I lost my confidence and became fearful of doing anything in front of Len in case he would find fault." Unwittingly Alice no longer sent messages to Len that he was better than anyone else. In response, she sensed his supreme effort to be superior. She

_____ Susan R. Shapiro and Michele Kasson, Ph.D.

retreated into her shell, realizing he no longer found her exciting and fun. "My feelings seemed to hold no accountability. Len saw my career as worthless and my close friendships with women to be ridiculous and demanding. Whenever I spent time with a woman friend, he became angry, saying I chose her over him. I started to realize we were not connected at all."

IS THERE TRUE EMPATHY?

The narcissist at the extreme has little emotional capacity for empathy. He will be disdainful of your differences. He will be convinced you are pushing him away. He may belittle you, demolishing your self-esteem.

Alice is still adjusting to this loss. "I'm relieved. I no longer have difficulty breathing. But I'm also in agony from the rejection. I feel the rug was pulled out from under me and I don't know why. I hear that he is dating with a fury while I'm healing. Although I miss him terribly, I see it is the illusion I crave, not Len."

Women need to gain insight into their attraction to this kind of man. If you are subdued, you may be attracted to a narcissist in order to live vicariously through him. If you would not buy showy clothing, fancy cars for yourself, you might love the gifts and acclaim that befall you. *If you can accept your own narcissistic needs to a greater extent, you will decrease your need to live through a mate.*

His motivation is to show his perfection to others and to be admired for his

---

HIS VIEW OF THE WORLD

He is the center of the universe

He has not outgrown his sense of being privileged and entitled

He is not a team player

He requires you to agree to his agenda

success. In a relationship, he needs someone who can make others think highly of him. A beautiful trophy woman on his arm lets the world know of his achievements, functioning in much the same way as the flaunting of other expensive toys and signs of wealth.

We have to ask ourselves why we want a narcissist. Surely he is glamorous and charming. The successful narcissist is smooth and exudes a pervasive sense of well being. His is nonchalant and cool, unflustered and in control of the situation. Underneath this veneer is his need for constant attention, a belief in entitlement and a fantasy of his own self-worth. He is exploitative of others, as evidenced in Alice and Len's story, and feels his own self-importance. He will shower you with gifts but only to show you how swell he is. Once he has you where he wants you, there is no need to maintain the charade. When you realize who this man is, and his efforts no longer have an effect, his gifts will no longer be forthcoming.

WHO IS A NARCISSIST/DISARMER?

A narcissist is egocentric and needs others to bolster a false sense of self. He avoids his own feelings of inadequacy. His impressive exterior covers up an inadequate interior. The exterior needs to be constantly inflated. The adoration of others protects his ego.

It takes a woman quite some time to get to this place, where she understands who she is dealing with. His interest in you prevails as long as you fulfill his needs. When you require a change to a more substantive relationship, his interest dissipates. A woman experiences this in a painful, belabored drama when the narcissist begins to disparage her, and no longer appreciates who she is. The narcissist views a

_____ Susan R. Shapiro and Michele Kasson, Ph.D.

woman as an object of desire, if brief desire. She constitutes a part of him, the piece that he feels is lacking in himself.

REPEAT PERFORMANCE

Once you have been involved with a narcissist/disarmer, the question to be asked is will you seek out another? Despite the pain it has caused, will you idealize the next partner, hoping this time that his admiration can last?

Life is thrilling for a woman who is entangled with a narcissist. The environment is exciting, and energized, like a story book. It seems too good to be true at the start. Eventually a woman longs for the relationship to grow in a meaningful way. She seeks an emotional depth, a true give and take between partners, which may be difficult due to the narcissism.

When Jody, at forty, met Bill, who was thirty-nine, she identified with his extreme talent as an actor/musician. Jody interpreted that he was not interested in a material life, but one in which he was appreciated for his own gifts. "I didn't understand that Bill used his art as a way to avoid meaningful relationships. I admired him for his talent and had terrific empathy for his struggle to succeed in a very competitive world. It took me a long time to realize I was there to bolster his ego."

Jody, a teacher, admired Bill greatly, thus making him feel worthy. "Bill drew me into his world, and I appreciated that. Because we lived in New York City, he took me to theater events and constant parties, where I felt I was

ARE YOU HIS IDEAL MATE?

Can you tolerate his contempt for others?
If his companions are not ideal, his image is deflated
If the mirroring is not adequate, he is unhappy, and takes it out on you

alive. I suppose I was seduced—he was a fabulous ballroom dancer and dazzled me with his charm. I was this solid, daily worker, who cared about my students, and I knew that my life was mundane by comparison to Bill's. He swept me off my feet but then I began to see things differently. He was definitely on the cutting edge of style and savior faire, but everything about his world was deliberate and premeditated."

At the start, Jody could do no wrong in Bill's eyes. "Bill was compelled to show me off to his friends as a fine addition. I was on his arm, the perfect mate. He always had to be the best and I suppose I suited his needs. I don't think that Bill deceived himself consciously, but for anything negative in his life, he made excuses and blamed others. It was never his fault."

> **ARE YOU FALLING FOR THIS MAN?**
> *Do you find yourself lost to his charming ways?*
> *Do you admire him as the center of attention?*
> *Are you on a pedestal without knowing why?*
> *Does he seem to be superior to others?*
> *Does he deprecate those who don't see him as special?*
> *Is he a rule breaker?*
> *Does he reciprocate favors?*
> *Is he self-important even when he captivates you?*
> *Does he manipulate his co-workers to his own benefit?*

Slowly, Jody began to find that Bill's way of life was interfering with her own life. "I was too tired from the late nights to be able to concentrate on my own work. The mutual adoration began to dwindle when I explained to him that I was ready to cut down on the late night scene. What was fun at the start had become more of the same. The same faces night after night, and the same struggles began to bother me. I explained that my needs had to be accounted for but Bill would not address these issues. Instead he began to dimish my life and told me that what I wanted was not significant."

LIFE ON HIS TERMS

He patronizes you as long as he desires your attention—this could last a lifetime. Because he is there only for himself his commitment to you may be superficial.

Sex, which at the outset was intense and romantic for Jody and Bill, had changed also. No more did Bill initiate unending hours of love making. "I missed the intimacy. Those evenings where Bill danced me around the table were gone. He had set the stage and then let it go. I began to suspect this was his pattern with all women. He even confessed that the dancing and wining and dining had been a part of each of his previous relationships. I realized that it was not about a particular woman for Bill. It seemed as if every relationship was the same for him, except that the woman changed. I panicked."

The relationship began to fall apart. "Bill had never wanted to please me or to be there for me. He was simply presenting himself as doing all of the right things, but it always seemed superficial. I began to be more and more isolated, but I couldn't put my finger on why I felt so uncomfortable. There was no time to be with my own friends and I worried because I was not connecting to Bill's friends. I thought that it was me"

The narcissist/disarmer's universe is constructed and arranged so that he is always reinforced, and feels secure. His sincerity and goodness seem a sham as his grandiosity rises to the surface. The woman feels deceived. His relationships are circumscribed. It is when his partner searches for more substance that the narcissist/disarmer gets into trouble.

Jody was able to convince Bill that they should be in therapy. "We decided to try to make a go of the relationship, hoping to regain the feelings we had in the beginning. At the first session Bill said he was unaware of any problem in the relationship other than my moodiness and unhappiness. I said he had abandoned me. He was so charming to the therapist, trying to win him over with his wit and manner. He would not talk about his feelings or issues concerning the relationship. I knew he saw it as a waste of time. I knew he would not go back. Bill had no intention of changing any of his behaviors. Bill informed me that the therapist was no good, and would not be able to help. He said that I should stop seeing this phony. I was beside myself, but there was nothing more to do."

Bill moved on, picking up his life where he left off, distracting himself with his previous activities. Jody continued with the therapist, trying to understand how such a life together could fall apart with no warning to her, no apparent reason. In time, she learned about her motivations for choosing a man like Bill.

YOUR MOTIVATIONS

A narcissist will resonate against your personal weakness. He needs you to inflate him, and you become caught up in the grand illusion. If you stay with this man, the perceptions change. Everything wrong becomes your fault.

Desiree's encounter with a narcissist/disarmer led her to her second marriage. Gregory, thirty-five, and Desiree, forty-two, met at a coffee bar in Seattle. Desiree was divorced with one child and working long hours as a club manager. Initially she was quite smitten with him. "I thought that Gregory was exuberant, charming, outgoing and passionate. He was the flip side of my incredibly sedate first husband. What I didn't know until I had given birth to our first child was that he was truly spoiled, narcissistic, emotionally abusive and destructive. The level of anxiety was intolerable. He was both verbally and physically abusive, yet at times quite loving. I never knew what was coming."

Desiree recognized that her husband was out of control and very dependent on her. As in many situations with a narcissistic partner, Gregory did well with the relationship until he became a father. He could not make the transition from center stage to the periphery as the baby demanded Desiree's attention. When family members came to visit the baby, Gregory took all the glory and Desiree was exiled to the kitchen. In hopes of improving the marriage by solidifying the family, Desiree gave birth to their second child twenty months after the birth of their first. "I think he needed something I had. I sensed something was very wrong in the marriage, but I hoped that these babies would hold us together."

The evolution of family life did not sit easily with Gregory who needed a carefree lifestyle. Coming home to face the drudgery, he felt imprisoned. To further complicate things, his career which was ascending began to diminish. "My husband was devastated when his work fell apart. That was when his nature actually revealed itself. Had he not become abusive at that time, I might have stayed not realizing how dangerous his actions were to me. There were other issues. I remained attracted to him throughout, and he could still be extremely charismatic and magnetic. He remained the life of the party, and was always fun. While he was gregarious in public, in private he was brooding, moody, negative and sarcastic. Always I was the object. If we were sitting in traffic, it was my fault. He was always pushing the limits, there were no boundaries."

In any long term relationship, there is the hope that the early qualities can be recaptured. For this reason, many women like Desiree remain and attempt to ignore the problems. "I would have stayed but the abuse escalated. I was hurt physically and I finally got a court order. By then I was finished loving him and afraid of him. I remained disappointed for years that we were unable to solve our issues and could not heal the wounds. Today I am back on my feet, I have a job and the children are in good shape. It was a journey.

"Now when I meet a man I know what to avoid and what to appreciate. I am still attracted to the charismatic type that my ex-husband was, but I've become more self protective. I seek respect, civility, tenderness and someone who considers my needs and the children's without my asking."

WHEN HE LASHES OUT

A narcissist/disarmer will feel trapped in a situation where he is expected to give emotionally. Being a breadwinner is acceptable because it is not about feelings and the outside world respects him. If his career dissolves and other demands are placed upon him, he may lose it.

In a less negative mode, Pamela was able to enjoy her relationship with Alex while understanding its limits. "Because I was in my forties, and he was in his early thirties and wanted children, we both understood it was not to be a long standing liaison. We stayed together one year. There was lots of sex in the beginning and lots of attention paid to me. I thought that I clung to him long after it was over because I was the older woman. The truth is that I clung because he wasn't really there."

Pamela and Alex cooked together, attended sports events and movies, and shared most weekend time together. However, the relationship was mostly sexual with a strong physical connection. "I absolutely craved him. It was the first time in my life I ever felt like that. In truth, he was selfish, the world revolved around him, and he was very spoiled. His life was the gym, his work as an attorney, and making enough money to support his lifestyle without thinking of anyone else. My schedule, as an art gallery owner, revolved around his. He was inflexible and I was flexible."

Three years later Alex is not married, despite his great claim to desire a wife and children. "My take on it is that he couldn't tolerate the attention they would eat up. We had to do whatever he wanted, whenever he wanted to, and the way that he wanted to. I always would succumb to his wishes." When this relationship had come to a natural ending, Pamela was grateful for the time spent with Alex. "He made me feel glamorous and young. He was an intelligent and exciting man. Just not for the long haul."

> **MAKING IT WORK**
>
> If you feel you cannot live without your narcissist/disarmer be prepared for:
>
> *A seesaw existence*
> *To be adored or ridiculed*
> *Financial, but not emotional care taking*
> *Social customs tossed to the wind*
> *A less than full partnership*

Ceci is a forty-seven year old journalist who lives in Washington, D.C. with her two college-age children. Previously divorced, she was widowed three years ago. "My second marriage came after a whirlwind courtship. He had money and power, but it was his narcissistic nature that was notable. I understood this about him, and I thrived on it. I craved his attention and lived for the good days. I would do it again. He was unpredictable—either I was on his side and it was us against the world or I was his enemy and the recipient of his dark mood. Yet we were very close and he was very loyal to me in his own way. I saw my husband, Todd, as very needy underneath. He needed to be the center of attention at all times."

Ceci realized that Todd could be infantile and accepted his behavior. She internalized her unhappiness and chose not to confront him. "I did not feel there were options or I never considered the options. He was verbally abusive and still I knew that he loved me, he had to have me there. People saw him as arrogant and yet he was very charismatic. My children loved him and he was a good stepfather to them."

> **HOW TO SURVIVE THE NARCISSIST/DISARMER**
> *Protect any chink in your armor*
> *Remember the choice to be there is yours*
> *Verify your self-esteem through other sources*
> *Make your needs known—definitively but gently*
> *Assuage his fear of abandonment*

After nine years of marriage, Ceci's husband contracted terminal cancer. "I only knew that he was ill and would die. I must have wanted him dead subconsciously because I knew that death was a way out. I would never have considered divorce. Besides, fifty percent of the time, I did not want a way out. I never considered leaving. His illness was terribly frightening to me. I stayed beside him because he required it of me. My first husband had been quite absent and Todd was the real father to these children. We all wanted him to be in the picture despite his moods and rages."

As in the case with many narcissistic personalities, Todd's extraordinary generosity went a long way. "I was showered with gifts . That was on a good day. On a bad day, I knew that when he walked in the door he'd been in a rage and that it was my fault even if it was about the weather. The circumstances had nothing to do with me although he saw me as responsible. Everything was my fault. I had more power than the President of the United States. I know that I did not want to give up the power he imbued me with. No one wants to give up that kind of power. He was powerful with everyone else and I was powerful with him. I enabled him and he claimed he would not have been who he was without me. After two years of raging cancer, he died."

The power play which Ceci describes in her entanglement with her narcissist/disarmer is common. There were days when the lifestyle and excitement were enough to keep her there and days when Todd's behavior and anger tossed her to the depths. In a relationship with a narcissistic personality, the woman lets her partner know it is her choice to leave or stay. It is she who prevails.

Narcissistic personality characteristics can be extreme or mild. For Alison, who is forty-three and lives in a suburb of Detroit, her final relationship was with a man who exhibited these traits to a lesser extent. After dating her second husband for four months they decided to marry. Alison had two children from her first marriage as did Samuel. Together they have one child.

"I fell madly in love with Samuel. He was good to my children but not great. After several years of dating, I realized that I could take advantage of what he was willing to offer and fill in the rest myself. I knew that he was narcissistic in nature and a strong, successful, handsome man. He was very appealing yet I knew that he could be selfish and materialistic. I recognized the differences between him and my first husband. This man is not as fine a person. He is always telling me what to do. He always makes me feel he is more important than me because he works and I'm not working at present. He tries to demean me and humiliate me. I know how to deal with him within the constraints, so I'm on top of the situation. To this day I realize that my first husband is a kinder and more generous man.

"Life was easier with my first husband but it is much more exciting and interesting with Samuel. We do sports together and his energy level is high. There is always humor and fun, and he is very smart. However, when he is good, it's fantastic and when he is in a funk, I have learned how to humor him. Samuel has come a long way in this marriage. We have worked together to bring about positive changes. I have learned to show him how good he is without subjugating myself. Both of us are interested in change and in making the marriage work. After the years we have shared, and having each gone through a divorce with children, it is worth it to overlook our idiosyncrasies. Whatever Samuel does that is narcissistic, he also gives a lot to the marriage."

> **HOW TO MAKE IT WORK**
> *Be willing to fight for half the spotlight*
> *Have the strength to stand up to his demands*
> *Make your interests as important as his*
> *Nurture him and nurture yourself*

2

*"I've done everything I know to try and make you mine, and
I think I'm going to love you for a long, long time."*
— Linda Rondstadt

AMBIVALENCE SYNDROME

An ambivalent man is in conflict and struggles to resolve the issue. In every aspect of his life he cannot decide to be dependent or independent. When it manifests in relationships, he finds he comes forward and then backs away. A relationship with this type of man causes the partner to feel uneasy and unsure of where she stands. His moods shift unpredictably and his pessimism is almost always apparent in one form or another. Throughout history the plight of the ambivalent man has been shown to us repeatedly. The most obvious of the moment is that of Prince Charles. In love with a married woman, Camilla Parker Bowles, he attempted to create and sustain a marriage to Diana. Finally his ambivalence was resolved and the arduous decision to divorce was announced to the world. While none of us has the royal responsibilities of Prince Charles, a similar scenario can be found in the ambivalent men described in our book. Torn and uncertain, their personalities are altered by the weight of indecision. They become restless and unpredictable as a result, and the woman who is at their mercy is in a state of great upset.

One such prominent figure was that of Aristotle Onassis, who maintained a relationship with Maria Callas, the opera diva, while he was married to Jacqueline Kennedy. Thus Onassis represents a man who made the decision to marry but could not make the decision to extricate himself from his former lover. In literature, this theme recurs. An excellent example is Colleen McCullough's best selling novel, *The Thorn Birds*, the story of a man's ambivalent love for the church and for a woman. Ultimately he chooses the church, but is filled with anguish and unrest the remainder of his days. We read in Milan Kundera's novel, *The Unbearable Lightness of Being*, of a poignant triangle between Tomas, a neurosurgeon, his wife, Tereza, and his lover, Sabina. Tomas spends much of his life ambivalent and undecided, traveling between the two women.

On a less serious note, the film *Heartbreak Kid* tells the tale of a young man on his honeymoon who spots the woman of his dreams. Despite the vows he has just taken, he seeks out his fantasy, and abandons his marriage. Once immersed in the life which the fantasy woman offers, he longs for the life that he originally found satisfying. In Jane Austen's novel and in the recent film, *Sense and Sensibility*, we find the heroines' hearts set on certain men. These potential mates, who are granted great power, are conflicted as to which woman will prove worthy of them. The heroines, through perseverance and self-esteem, end up the victors.

Susan R. Shapiro and Michele Kasson, Ph.D.
KNOW YOUR MAN

If we compare the ambivalent man to the narcissistic man we see how unique the situations are. The ambivalent man has two women because he is unable to make a choice while the narcissistic man believes he deserves both.

We have described the narcissist/disarmer as a man who deceives himself and others with an unrealistically inflated persona. He flaunts social conventions because he feels that he is above such rules due to his inherent superiority. He sees himself at the center of the universe, and solely considers his feelings, while lacking empathy for the feelings of others. Frequently, his behavior exploits anyone with whom he interacts. *This is not the case with the ambivalent man. Yet like the narcissist, he is unable to display deeper emotions to his significant other.* This occurs for an array of reasons.

Deidre, at the age of forty-nine, has recently left a relationship with ambivalent man who claimed he wanted to remarry, but in truth was unable to decide. "Jim was a doctor who had been married for over twenty-five years. His wife had left him. When he met me he told me that I was his happiness. That was the hook for me, I fell for it. What I didn't know was that he didn't feel that he deserved to be so happy. We were together through his sister's death and I stood beside him. He made me feel important and appreciated. Later on his true colors began to show. He would treat me one way and then completely change his tune. He could be very difficult and I knew this was ill fated. For all of the times that he claimed he wanted me to be his second wife, I had a terrible feeling it could not be. Finally he could not decide."

Ultimately, Deidre grieved for the loss of the relationship. She realized too late that had she better understood

Jim's behavior, she might have stayed. When the time together became too painful, she gave up. "It was the pulling close and pushing me away that was intolerable. Things should have gotten better but instead he purposely made things difficult. He wanted to bury his head. Instead of turning to me, he turned against me."

THE WOMAN IN HIS LIFE

Often in this syndrome the woman stands dutifully at her partner's side while he is contrary and ambivalent. There is always the hope that the good will surface. The women who seek him out are left hungry for more.

The ambivalent man is undecided in his feelings toward himself and toward others. Because he is unsure of his own needs, he acts impulsively. Without self-knowledge, this ambivalent man takes action on the spur of the moment. For instance, he will make a choice against his desires. The expression, "You always hurt the one you love" applies here, even if it is inadvertent. This man is torn and tormented. He does not know what he wants and cannot make a decision about who he wants. Not feeling justified, his entire being is filled with doubt, guilt, and apprehension due to his deceit. He often makes sure that his partner finds out about the duality in hope that the decision will be made for him.

Sally met Roger while at a New Age retreat. "He was the opposite of my husband, very warm and seemingly open. He listened to everything I had to say and took a tremendous interest in my well being. He appeared to be available, and interested in my spiritual awakening. What grew out of friendship was a love affair, but always there was something lurking, something amiss. He would get

_____ Susan R. Shapiro and Michele Kasson, Ph.D.

very close and then distance himself without ever losing the caring. This pattern went on for two years, I could not put my finger on it."

Sally discovered that Roger hid behind his spiritual beliefs, which were in opposition to his high powered career. As he became more unavailable, his actions and beliefs contradicted each other. "If only I had understood that Roger's dilemma was all internalized. He professed to be open and honest. He was elusive and omitted important details. And then it became a slow dawning. He, in fact, could not decide between me and another woman."

The more that Roger danced toward and away from Sally, the more she wanted him. Eventually he confessed that his other relationship was not happy, but that he suffered a keen sense of obligation. "I was devastated and betrayed. My ex-husband had been loyal and his behavior had been stable. This was the flip side — for everything that Roger told me there was another aspect to the story that was not revealed. In a desperate attempt to hold the relationship together, I confronted him. I knew that we shared something unique and special. He was so unsure of what to do. While we were in the middle of it all, he told my friends that it was me that he loved. Yet in the end he chose her. He continues to tell people that he is not going to marry her. Had he remained with me, we would have been married. Obviously he couldn't make that choice. With the other woman he does not have to."

ARE YOU PREY TO AN AMBIVALENT MATE?

Are his moods unpredictable?
Does he procrastinate?
Is he a chronic complainer?
Does he put you on edge?
Is he pleasant even when he disappoints you?
Does he disappear on occasion?
Does he kill you with kindness?

Since Sally was strong enough to resist an unsatisfying relationship with Roger, she was able to go forward with her life. Roger's altruism and self-sacrifices were appealing initially for Sally in her vulnerable, newly divorced state. Often women are manipulated by these traits and unwittingly remain in a bad situation for years.

Jackie's enduring connection to an ambivalent man has recently ended. The most significant characteristic of her relationship was his method of criticizing her.

In the guise of friendly concern, Patrick was hypercritical and unsupportive of Jackie. "Patrick's criticism of me was always couched in the most loving terms. He was adamant about how I should conduct my life. When my youngest child was in kindergarten, he failed to recognize my desire to re-enter the workplace. He was not outspoken about it, rather he insinuated that I was a poor mother for wanting this. I spent so much time feeling as if I was doing the wrong thing. And it was not even his child. Patrick was unsettled about his own life and career. Perhaps that colored his view of mine."

HOW HE OPERATES

When offered, the ambivalent man's intelligence and sensitivity are most appealing. Unfortunately these same qualities can be used to his partner's disadvantage. This type of man may employ guilt and manipulation to achieve his ends.

The scenario with many ambivalent men is that they take their conflict out in their relationships. The woman who becomes attached to such a man may feel deceived and extremely let down. The nature of the beast is one where he may seem empathic and extremely thoughtful. In reality he may be much too entrenched in his own hellish world to react on more than a superficial basis to yours.

_____ Susan R. Shapiro and Michele Kasson, Ph.D.

In the case of Angela, who was thirty-six when she met her ambivalent mate at work, there was the perception that he would find his way. Because Peter was fairly honest about the fact that he was dating both Angela and another woman, Angela believed that she would prove the winner. "For eighteen months Peter and I spent many nights together, becoming close as friends and lovers. While the sex was important to the relationship, it was the friendship that drove it home. He was so kind to me when my brother died and I honestly do not think I could have gotten through it without him. If there was any kind of crisis at all, Peter was there."

When asked if Peter was available on a day to day basis, for the mundane in life, Angela paused, and had to think. "He seemed present all the time because there was always a crisis. And always there was the other woman, and the eventual contest. Someone had to win and I clearly believed it was going to be me. She did not even know about me, and I knew that theirs was not a love match, but something he felt beholden to. In retrospect, Peter needed to be a savior and this woman had continual scenes in her life."

Peter's profile exemplifies how easy it is to rise to someone else's occasion when one's own life is in turmoil and unreconciled. In order to function, the ambivalent man shifts his focus to those of lesser importance or power, giving him a sense of greater control of his own life. With Angela's story, there appeared to be an issue of religion. Yet Angela knew that this was used as an excuse. "Peter did marry her, and he broke my heart. He took me out to lunch to explain the reason. When he told me it was one of religion I knew that he simply could not make up his mind and had taken the easier route. I would have converted. He knew that. They had known each other for so many years that when she made her final plea he impulsively agreed.

His ambivalence was so great that they were married within a few days. I know that had a wedding date been set, it would have been canceled."

Peter's fears manifested in his accusation that Angela could not be there for him, while the woman he married would always be there. In reality, Peter was expressing his own insecurities about failing Angela. His trepidation was acted out explicitly in his spur of the moment marriage. Quite frequently there is a more passive manner of acting out, and it is not as obvious as in Angela's story. The salient point here is that this man is not who he seems at the outset because of his own paradox.

WHO IS THE AMBIVALENT MAN ?

This man will listen to your tale of woe even as he feels misunderstood and unappreciated. Unsure of who he is, he hides himself. He feels cheated of opportunity and taken advantage of in life, but may not express it. Until the ambivalence surfaces, you may feel quite good being with him.

The setting for Claudia and David to meet was perfect. They began dating during a summer vacation and soon were in love in their home town of Baton Rouge. There was instant chemistry and compatibility. At the age of forty- seven and recently divorced, Claudia had not anticipated meeting anyone. David, on the other hand, was extricating himself from what he described as a seven year failed relationship. After the vacation the new lovers spent numerous days together, always happily. The pace of the relationship was rapid and not confined to weekends. They dated seriously and supposedly exclusively for two years. By coincidence one day, Claudia ran into David on the street. He was with another woman and clearly they were attached.

"David ducked into a store, advising this woman to go ahead. I was in shock. I followed him in and confronted him, because I could not believe my eyes. David told me that I was crazy, that nothing was going on. He said we'd have to speak later that day. I thought that David and I were totally one—and I had not seen anything in his attitude to make me believe otherwise. I'd had an unhappy marriage and really cherished our playful and wonderful friendship. David always seemed to be so steady. I did not allow myself to see anything in his personality to make me think that this would not work out."

It was only when Claudia had a conversation with David's close friend that she began to understand what was going on. In a typical ambivalent man syndrome, David was unable to decide between two women and the kind of life each offered him. As the story unfolded, Claudia discovered that the other woman had begun to date David ten years earlier while David was still married. The second woman was never apprised of the fact that David was now divorced. She continued to believe that she was dating a married man. It was this lie that enabled David to date both Claudia and his long time lover. In the face of his own needs, David was willing to fool and jeopardize the lives of two women. This was not the case of a man who wanted it all, but the case of a man who did not know what he wanted.

Claudia decided to leave the relationship. "I learned from our mutual friend that David had been urged by those who knew the entire situation to make a choice. He simply could not do it. His anguish was nothing compared to his inability to come to a decision. I suppose he wanted to end up with one or the other but he was tortured. I could not abide it."

Unlike the ambivalent men who have difficulty in

choosing a relationship, we also see ambivalence taking the form of passive-aggressive behaviors with others. When mild, the negativity observed is barely noticeable. However, in extreme situations, there can be tremendous negativity. These men are no longer fun to be with. They sulk, complain, and ruin the party. They can be contrary and unpredictable, pessimistic, irritable, and will undermine your pleasure. Life with such a person can be difficult because of his moodiness, restlessness, and impatience.

REMEMBER: *The ambivalent man lets his partner learn of the duality in hope that she will decide for him.*

Niki, a make-up artist, at the age of thirty-six, has been intimately involved with Craig, a never-married private investigator, who is five years her junior. At first he was attentive and sensitive to Niki. Today she feels he is extremely ambivalent about the relationship. "He rarely arrives on time and blows hot and cold in terms of his feelings. Just when I think everything is good and solid, he backs off. Craig tells me I'm smothering him. When we talk about getting married, or about a monogamous relationship, he agrees that's what he wants, but I get this feeling it's lip service. It's not the way I imagined it would be with my children, either. He's okay with them, but there's no real bonding. I don't care anymore—they have

> **HOW TO SURVIVE YOUR AMBIVALENT MAN**
> *Be prepared for his moodiness*
> *Let him know that you understand his mixed feelings*
> *Provide a safe harbor for him*
> *Show him that you won't disappoint him*
> *Encourage his independent thinking*

_____ Susan R. Shapiro and Michele Kasson, Ph.D.

a father. Craig says that he wants more children, and he knows I would also. Then he says nothing about it for weeks at a time. In the past year it's been difficult to spend time with him. I never know what his mood will be when he walks through the door. He no longer seems up, but down about things. These days I don't know what he is thinking. Out of nowhere he will become nasty or stubborn. I know he can't make up his mind about us, and that's why he's so hard to be with. There are a lot of qualities about him that I love. I plan to stick it out."

> **TELLTALE SIGNS OF THE AMBIVALENT MAN**
>
> *He is uneasy when you mention a future date*
> *He seems to be keeping a secret*
> *The conversations are more about your life than his*
> *He break dates frequently*
> *You have not met his friends. His life is kept apart from your time together*

Mae, at the age of thirty-eight, and separated from her husband, began a passionate relationship with Vince, a contractor who she met through business. He was twenty-nine at the time, and seemed "very together". He hesitated initially, and Mae did not understand why. "I knew there was this instant attraction. He kept it at arm's length for months. One day, we ended up at the same party, and he professed great love for me. I was swept off my feet. The crisis of my impending divorce was such that I really needed his support. I didn't learn who he really was, I was so busy talking about me. Later, I discovered that he was engaged to someone in a nearby town. Then his ambivalence surfaced—he could not decide who he wanted."

Because Vince was so troubled by his conflicting feelings, he allowed Mae to know of his fiancee. Vince's need to confide was a way of asking Mae to help him make a decision. It is almost as if he needed Mae to tell him what he really wanted. As soon as the conflict became overwhelming to him, his personality changed around Mae. "He became obsessed, demanding, possessive. The man I thought was kind, giving, and religious and wouldn't date clients was like a fatal attraction. He was so jealous, even though I wasn't the one to be jealous of. We would be going out with friends to have a good time. Without warning, his mood would become foul, putting everyone on edge. I did not know what kind of person he would be when we arrived somewhere. He could still be sociable, but these events were far and few between. I was choking.

"The fiancee was the person I really pitied—he said that he was planning to break it off with her but neglected to tell her. In fact, I don't think he ever planned to tell her. Vince hadn't a clue as to who he really wanted. What was so difficult to understand was how good the good was. When the love was in place, it was the kind of love people only dream about."

Mae eventually left Vince and began to date, feeling she had gotten away relatively unscathed. However, to this day she misses the closeness and the support that Vince offered.

Ivy met Timothy at a bar in Sante Fe on her fortieth birthday. He told her immediately that he had never been married and that he had never met anyone that he felt he could marry. He told Ivy that he was thirty-nine years old and worked for a large corporation. "In retrospect, everything that he said was a lie. He did not really have a job after having been fired. He began to stay with me every night although he said he had an apartment about half an hour away. Every day I dropped him off at his supposed office and I went on to my work as a designer. He knew where I lived and worked but I knew nothing about him,

_____ Susan R. Shapiro and Michele Kasson, Ph.D.

as I think back. He was sweet, gentle and kind. I was in love with him although I did not know enough about him. We spent most nights together and this lasted for over a year."

One evening Ivy came out of the bedroom to find Timothy chopping cocaine on her dining room table. She was mortified and hurt, and kicked him out. "Whenever we had arguments, he'd send me bouquets of flowers. This time I resisted a bit longer after the flowers arrived, but basically it was another scene and then a reunion. As I think back I assume that he took coke or dealt coke the entire time we were together. I became suspicious of him, despite the flowers and his sweetness. I had my friend follow his car one day and I learned that he had a wife and children. I confronted him and told

> **COMPROMISING POSITIONS/ REMAINING WITH AN AMBIVALENT MAN**
>
> *He struggles to feel good about his choice*
> *He may not be steady in work or as a partner*
> *He can be sullen and moody*
> *His half truths will haunt you.*

him to bring me divorce papers. He said he could not leave that life totally but wanted me. And what about that first night, when he told me that he was never married? This man had children, and he had lied to me. I suspect that the flowers that were sent to me were charged to someone else's account. His entire existence was a lie. So while I thought that we were close, I knew nothing of this man. We never spoke of marriage but this man definitely loved me. I was always happy when I was with him. I knew that he had this other life, that he couldn't make up his mind about something big, but I chose to ignore it, to see how time would take care of things."

Ivy allowed her ambivalent man enough space. One

morning when she dropped him off at his purported job, she looked in her rear view mirror and saw him staring at her intently. This was the last time that she ever saw him. "He simply disappeared. I tried to track him down and learned later on that he'd gone abroad. I suspect he was in some kind of trouble. I don't know how to trust another man...to believe what he says to me after Timothy. I was totally deceived."

WHEN HE LIES TO YOU

The ambivalent man believes his own lies. He is in turmoil and views his story as a necessity, a mollifier. He wants you when he wants you until he doesn't want you.

Jessica, at the age of thirty-five, had been married for ten years when her husband began having an affair. Despite the problems inherent to the marriage, she was deeply hurt and betrayed by this discovery. She confronted Thomas, who admitted that he did not want to give up his lover nor did he want to be divorced. Having been ambivalent about his career for years, Jessica saw Thomas' inability to make this decision simply one more manifestation of his ambivalence.

"I knew he would beg me to stay and that I would not be able to trust him to leave her. He kept telling me it was over and I would learn that it wasn't. I wanted my marriage to succeed. I wanted to have children and to have a life with Thomas. We spoke about it at length. I told him that he had to make a decision. He wanted us both, and yet he knew I would not stay under that circumstance. Finally, after months and months of back and forth, he decided to remain in the marriage. Today we still have our problems, but I am pregnant and I do believe that Thomas is here to stay. I'm pleased that I did not let it end over the affair. I know that when he met me there was someone in his life. I suppose that this is his pattern. He has come to terms with it, I hope this time it is for good."

Never married and thirty-five, Patricia works as a police dispatcher in Tallahassee, Florida. She has been in love with Glen, a married man for the past two years, always with the hope that he will leave the marriage. "I know that he does not love his wife and that he feels beholden to her. For all this time we have been meeting at hotels and sneaking around. But she knows about us and I think he wants her to know. He wants her to kick him out. He wants someone else to make the decision for him. And at the same time, he can't give her up and he can't give me up. He wants us both. His marriage has never been happy but he stays for the children."

> ## INDEPENDENCE VS. DEPENDENCE
> *He wants you to take care of him, but he yearns to be free.*
> *He desires your children but wishes you childless.*

Not only is Patricia's lover unhappy with his marriage, but he is not secure or grounded in his career. "This man has had several jobs in eighteen months' time. He can't seem to find something that he likes. This is very worrisome to me. He is afraid to make a decision and afraid to be on his own. He's anxious about everything. He is driving a taxi now, but he used to drive a bus and before that he worked for a limo company. None of it made him feel good about himself. He tells me I make him feel good about things but he won't take action on the rest of his life. And his wife must have some kind of hold over him. He loves his kids and when he is away from them he becomes cranky and miserable. Frankly I don't even want him around. I get the feeling that when he is with me, he wants them and when he's with his family and wife, he wants me. I want a full life and someone to be there. Recently I told Glen that he has to make a choice. If he can't leave his wife, then he'll stay and I'll have to get over it. I have a feeling as long as he's with her, he'll be looking for me to fill in the emptiness. I don't want to be caught in this trap anymore."

Not all ambivalencies manifest in triangles. Ambivalent men may exhibit their confusion in a relationship which involves only the two partners. In these cases, there are often shades of the narcissist/disarmer and the commitment phobic, as well as the ambivalent man. Sydney and Dan were in such a mode in a relationship which began on a most promising note. When they met through mutual friends, Sydney was warned that Dan had been through many trysts and was finally ready for the real thing. Sydney, thirty-eight, was divorced for two years and the mother of twin daughters, age seven. Her ex-husband lived in Hawaii and was remarried. Dan, at forty-three, was divorced and childless. Sydney's schedule as a dance instructor was flexible, and enabled her to be available to her daughters after school. Dan, as an actuary, worked long hours. Both live in a beach community in Southern California.

"I was finally ready for a committed relationship. After all, my girls were getting older and more independent and I knew that I was on solid ground. When Dan and I were introduced, there was instant chemistry. I should have listened to my one friend who knew him and warned me that he did not get involved with women who had children. Then why had he bothered to take my number and to call me up? I was so taken with him. And he seemed to be with me too. After a few weeks of dating we decided to spend time only with each other. I was in heaven. We were so compatible—on so many levels, sexually, conversationally, in terms of values. We spent some fabulous days together. I thought I'd met the man of my dreams. Then the tough times began. Every time that Dan wanted to see me, I'd jump for him, even if it wasn't convenient for me. And I did not see or feel the same level of energy coming from him. I found myself getting sitters every time he demanded my presence and I was torn. I hated leaving my girls all those nights. It wasn't what I wanted."

Dan had seemed so willing to please Sydney in the beginning and then he became hesitant about putting anything on the calendar. "He started to give me mixed messages. It felt like he was playing with my mind. Then I understood that he didn't know what he wanted. Sometimes he told me that he wanted children and a family of his own. Other days he told me that he wanted to move back East and other times he told me that he needed a partner who could go on exotic vacations with him. Meanwhile, he did little with my children and I wondered what kind of father he would be. He never traveled anywhere and his greatest fantasy was that he could become a ski instructor because he loved to ski. It dawned on me that Dan was totally ambivalent about his own life. He inflicted pain because his promises had no meaning for him. It was like playing a game. No matter what he said, he wanted to be a bachelor. He couldn't even figure out his work—was it boring or challenging, did he want to toss it in for another kind of existence? I started to see myself as the anchored one, and I was irritated with his attention half the time and his withdrawal and total selfishness the other half."

Sydney was able to tell Dan that she had needs and wanted a true partner. After a year of desperately attempting to solve unsolvable issues, she faced the fact that Dan was too confused about himself to ever be available to her. It was her ability to leave that set her free.

Ambivalent men often make important life decisions impulsively. The inability to make the right choice, one which will further their lives and goals, is significant. Many times this man is expressing deep inner turmoil shown by erratic and vacillating moods. This behavior elicits a negative reaction from his partner, which creates greater anxiety for the ambivalent man. After several episodes of this he may become more self-protective. Not wanting to face disappointment, he never fully gives himself to another, nor can he reap the benefit of a rich relationship. Thus the stage is set. *If his relationships anticipate disappointment and frustration, he never truly becomes emotionally involved. Then the next step out of a monogamous relationship is not such a large step after all. It is this pattern which perpetuates the ambivalence. The women he seeks out are at his mercy. It is up to you to bring about resolution and end on a positive note.*

The anxious or depressed man, like the ambivalent man, is at the mercy of his inner feelings. His relationships with women are based on his neediness and fears. He is unavailable because he is responding to what is going on inside of himself. Thus he cannot respond to a woman because he is struggling against his own demons. Often his anxiety or depression is triggered by an episode in his life: the tendencies might have been there all along, a vulnerable quality lurking in the background. For many, it is a specific ordeal which brings it to the surface. While some people are anxious or depressed by nature, others are fine until there is an event that unravels their lives.

Susan R. Shapiro and Michele Kasson, Ph.D.
YOUR UNHAPPY MAN

If you choose to be with an anxious or depressed man, you must be the stronger partner. Motivating him is the key—suggest vacations, outings. Keep him busy.

Jasmine met Gerard when his career was in a nose dive. As a scientist with a large company, he had recently been accused of falsifying research. Jasmine, a magazine editor, knew nothing of his field, and was supportive but uneducated. "I liked Gerard but he was so depressed. He was totally preoccupied with what would happen to him. There were some days when he was in such a black mood. He awoke early every morning feeling anxious. Yet we had some bond beyond his problems. I tried to make him feel better and to comfort him. He is a good person and I know that the charges against him are unfair. As we wait for the outcome, we are growing closer, and are beginning to be a couple. It has been a very slow process. Sometimes I wish it would be over because I want to be with him in the way I know we can be. I feel the potential. He has to know that I'll be there regardless of what happens. This inspires great trust. I know that when his life improves he'll always trust me because I was there when he was down and out. I am totally committed and still Gerard has anxiety which, by itself, keeps me at a distance. My frustration is that I can't get to the core. He is ambivalent about us because of the turmoil in his life."

> **IS HE ANXIOUS OR DEPRESSED?**
> *Does he have a sadness about him?*
> *Does he have little energy to experience the joys of life?*
> *Is he apprehensive?*
> *Does he feel as though he deserves punishment?*
> *Does he feel like his life is in a rut?*

Different people react differently when faced with tremendous stress in their lives. For some, the anxiety or depression can be pervasive, and a more serious problem to deal with in your partner. Gerard's nature is to become withdrawn, sad, and to worry endlessly as he responds to life's demands. A man like Gerard will be difficult for the woman in his life to handle. He will come toward her or pull away based on his situational mood. However, his mood will improve once his life straightens out. Yet this style of meeting with adversity is not likely to disappear. In many circumstances the burden which society places on a man to succeed provokes a dire reaction when things do not go as planned.

Regardless of the determining factor in the ambivalent man's behavior, working it out is a tricky business. Perseverence in the face of his mixed signals can elicit the result you want.

CAN YOU SUCCEED WITH YOUR AMBIVALENT MAN?

Learn his patterns

Know his history

Give it a time limit

Be strong enough to make your needs known

Expect these needs will be met

3

"It is a truth universally acknowledged, that a single man in possession of a good fortune, must be in want of a wife."
— Jane Austen

INSTANT FAMILY MAN AND WIDOWERS

There are men out there who, contrary to popular belief, gladly welcome women into their lives. As evidenced in *Pride and Prejudice*, it is not only women who seek a life-long mate, but men who are after this security. In today's world, a long-time bachelor may wake up suddenly and desire a complete family. Men who came of age during the Vietnam era have often put off marriage and parenting in order to get on the success track. Twenty years ago, a man in his early forties would have been approaching mid-life. Today, fifty-five is deemed mid-life. A single man who is approaching this stage often feels the need to make up for lost time. So hell bent on establishing his goal, he is strikingly unaffected by an ex-husband or, in the case of a widow, the shadow of the deceased partner.

For a woman fortunate enough to meet such a mate, there may still be issues to address. What might not be realized initially is that certain men have dependent personality traits. These manifest in a marked need for social approval, along with the support and affection of others. This instant family man is in search of nourishment and a connection to a woman who is dependable. With these conditions met, he will feel content and at ease, presenting himself to others as affable, generous, cooperative, and pleasant to be around.

If his dependence on another person is not sated, this man can be withdrawn, anxious, tense, depressed, and sad. In order to have his needs met, he may be submissive, too compromising, and clingy. He would rather give in to your wishes than independently strive for his goals. This man wants to become enmeshed in your life. Your children are the children he never had. Your family is the family he dreams of. He hopes to have comfort and solace within the structure. He is in a hurry, especially in mid-life and has a sense of urgency.

When Gina, a thirty-eight year old high school teacher, met Rob, forty-two, an investment banker, at a party, she was five years out of her divorce. Rob was in the midst of an acrimonious divorce, and had just begun to date. "Rob seemed green. He was definitely new at the game and was shy, which appealed to me. We spoke briefly before discussing the fact that we each had two children. Rob was in tremendous pain because his future ex-wife had turned the children against him. He seemed genuinely interested in hearing about my kids.

"We began to date on weekends and very quickly he wanted to see me more often. I agreed, and even allowed him to meet the kids early on in the game. Maybe it was that I didn't want to leave them with a sitter, or simply that

> **A MAN WITH A MISSION**
> *He speaks of fulfillment*
> *He is totally sincere*
> *He is generous as a means to an end*
> *He embraces your existence*

he was so pleasant and friendly. All of us began to go places together, movies, the mall. From the start it was obvious that his own children would not be a part of the picture. It wasn't exciting but it was a

> ### THE INSTANT FAMILY MAN'S M.O.
> *He longs to be part of a unit*
> *He cannot separate you from the package*
> *He does not learn who you really are*
> *He cannot recognize your desires over his*

form of family. I liked this but I certainly missed the romantic element. Even on a Saturday night he would be happy to be with the kids. This was a new relationship after all, and I wanted some time with Rob without my children. If we weren't with my kids, which was rare, he was talking about his kids and about his divorce."

Gina began to feel slightly uneasy but could not articulate what the problem was. She had reached a point where she was quite competent in her role as a single mother. Although she enjoyed the sense of family which Rob offered and the presence of a male, she felt it overwhelmed the adult relationship. She began to make noises to Rob who really did not hear her. Gina asked Rob on several occasions if they could devote more time to each other exclusively. While he promised to do so, it never materialized. Finally, after a few months where Gina felt displeased, she told Rob that she did not want to continue seeing him.

> ### THE INSTANT FAMILY MAN WANTS IMMEDIATE GRATIFICATION
> *Your children are the children he is missing*
> *He craves the stability you represent*
> *He needs what you have—a family*
> *He is in a great hurry*

Rob was devastated by Gina's decision. He begged her

to reconsider and announced his feelings for her and for her children. He was sincere but she knew she could not continue as things were. When Rob refused to take no for an answer, Gina simply ignored him. His calls became more frequent and more desperate. He missed her and the children — and felt it was a double blow after the machinations of his pending divorce. Within a few weeks, Gina met someone else and began to date, feeling there was more potential for balance with this new man. Rob could not stand being away from Gina and the children. It took a very long time for him to relinquish his hope of reconciliation.

Tory had been divorced for two years when she met Stewart during a business meeting in Atlanta. At the time she was dating someone else and felt semi-committed. Stewart and she experienced "instant chemistry" and within weeks were seeing each other constantly. Stewart had two college-age children and seemed to genuinely enjoy Tory's six-year old. "There was enough garbage in this relationship to discourage me from the beginning. I saw that Stewart was not totally extricated from his ex-wife, and that his children had quite a hold on him. Yet he really seemed to want a new life. He was enchanted with me and with my daughter. After a year we began to live together. Stewart was begging me to marry him so that we could be a family. He really put us first."

For Tory, it seemed too good to be true. After a very painful divorce and two difficult years alone, she hesitated before accepting.

HOW TO SPOT THE INSTANT FAMILY MAN

He is eager to please you

When he hears you have children he doesn't balk

Loneliness and abandonment are his greatest fears

He is ready to marry and settle down

He has a strong vision of how family life should be

_____ Susan R. Shapiro and Michele Kasson, Ph.D.

"He made an offer I couldn't refuse—including buying the house of my dreams and sending my daughter to parochial school. I saw the trade off—he wanted us very much. I realized my role as the recipient. He was so kind to me that I had no choice but to make my family his."

Although the instant family man has many positive characteristics, this prototype is not for everyone. He can be boring and docile, and for a woman who likes excitement and adventure in her mate, this can be disappointing. At family gatherings this man will shine because he seeks reinforcement from others, especially relatives. It is all a part of his great desire to create a protective layer about him, in the

> **FATHER WITHOUT A CHILD/MIDLIFE CRISIS**
>
> *He awakens and discovers he is without a family*
> *His yearning can be sated at once — by your package*
> *He is prepared to revolutionize his life for the rewards*

form of a family. He will be charming, gregarious and solicitous. The woman who marries this man can thank her lucky stars, because she and her children are now taken care of. She may also feel there is a trade off. She has forfeited her spiritedness for security. The instant family man truly believes in some rendition of a white picket fence.

The man who Antonia encountered after three years as a single parent was desirous of the warmth and security of a family. "He was so anxious to get married and to father my child. I had been married twice already, and in my mid-thirties, I really couldn't afford to make another mistake. Chris was nine years older than I and had been single for years. I could see that his hourglass was running out. I also believe that he was in love with me. I went in and out of the relationship because I was not ready to make a commitment. I felt smothered. For every promise he made to father my child and

The Men Out There

> **A MAN WITH AN AGENDA**
> Does he plan for the entire family without consulting you?
> Has he become best buddies with your siblings and parents?
> Do you feel it is happening too fast?
> Do you mistrust his intentions?

provide for me, I felt like I was in jail. I didn't want to be the traditional wife and mother that he wanted. His background made him possessive and needy. He wanted to have a big family and kids, yesterday. He kept talking about our having a baby.

As Antonia and Chris reached an impasse, the connections became unhealthy. "He wanted to control my child, and that frightened me. I did not notice this until we had been together for over a year. I started to withdraw and to spend less time with him. He became another person. He was no longer outgoing. He became like a recluse and did not want to go out. So while he was like a father to my child, and an overall good person, I had to keep her away. Suddenly he became short tempered and possessive because I would not agree to marry him. It was like a kid having a temper tantrum. There was no way to reason with him. He was jealous of what I had but would not share with him. I couldn't help it, I had to protect my daughter. He was in it for himself and not for us. Ultimately it was wrong and I knew that I had to let it go."

THE RESCUER

The rescuer recognizes your vulnerability. A divorced woman with small children is often extremely fragile, alone and hurting. This is appealing to the instant family man whose sense of worth comes from aiding others. He plays the part of hero in saving you and your children. This appeals to a woman in need or a woman who is truly ready to commit.

_____ Susan R. Shapiro and Michele Kasson, Ph.D.

Recently Sharon met Bruce, a man who fell into the categories of both instant family man and widower. After a very unhappy relationship which had lasted for over two years, she was wary of someone with such specific requirements. "By our second date I was beginning to change my mind. I realized that this is a very good man who is focused. While that's not what I'm used to, I can appreciate it. It's almost frightening to be with a man who knows his priorities. He is not afraid of commitment but is the opposite. He has a home life and a child whose mother died when he was quite young. This man is definitely looking for a partner. There is no ex-wife with her own story and no nights and weekends designated to his son. He has his son all of the time. Bruce cannot afford to waste his time. He is motivated to get on with his life. He wants to be married again and to have more kids."

Remarriage often seems more enticing to widowers than to divorced men. In the case of a widower, he did not choose to be single, it was unavoidable. When a widower does find a partner, he has a history of a successful marriage and the drive to begin again. For some, it is also survival, he wants a partner to help him navigate his life, to establish a sense of security. He may anticipate the reality of being torn between his children and his new wife, who cannot possibly replace his children's mother. He is also totally committed to making a success of his new marriage. A widower has less complications to bring to his second marriage than does a divorced man. He yearns to share his life with

> **WIDOWERS AS WINNERS**
> *His marriage did not fail, he has a positive memory*
> *He believes in the institution of marriage*
> *Time is of the essence*
> *He is tolerant of your children and your situation*
> *Responsibility is not a deterrent*

another person and to have a companion. Yet there are undeniable issues that come with the territory, despite the intent.

Sharon noticed that Bruce paced the relationship cautiously. "I have been careful to let him do things as he likes. He will book every weekend and one night during the week. He asked me at the outset what I was looking for and I told him that I wanted someone very smart with backbone. He is intellectually challenging and I like that. I have also spoken with him of values. It feels as if we are equals and as if he'd be able to balance us and his kid. Still it remains to be seen. What I have learned is that he is serious. It isn't a game for him. He's been through too much. If this is to work out, Bruce will have to totally trust me with his child and also be ready to create a family for us. It's a long road."

SEEKING A NEW MATE

The widower desires a second chance. Many friends have abandoned him, threatened by their own fear of mortality. He does not like being single in a coupled world. He has not chosen the world of singles in mid-life but has been thrust into it. A partner will protect him from the isolation.

Many widowers had relied on their wives for their social calendar. These men never developed the skills to create a life beyond the office. Suddenly they are parenting solo and looking for a social life. It is extremely difficult and overwhelming for them. The idea of running about, as divorced men in mid-life frequently do, may not be an appealing solution. Initially the widower is in shock and aggrieved, and at this point has no interest in another woman. He then begins to yearn for companionship and for the lifestyle that was taken from him.

Mimi, at the age of forty-one, found herself widowed with three children. Because her husband had been sick for an entire year, she was prepared for her widowhood, but petrified at living life alone. After several months of mourning, Mimi slowly entered the world of singlehood. "Everyone surrounded me when my husband died and promised to be there. But they quickly evaporated and I found myself very alone with my three kids. They were little, ages eight to twelve and my first priority was to get them settled. Then I landed a part time job at the school library. That was a big deal for me, because I'd stopped working when my youngest child was born. I had no time to date and then I realized I'd better do something to re-enter the world."

Mimi dated a man for two years who had a child but was estranged from him. The relationship had many positive components but ultimately Mimi felt that they were not in synchrony. "I had been married my entire adult life. I never expected to have a relationship that failed, that did not succeed. I suppose I had to get it over with. Then I dated for a while and that was how I met my present husband. We were introduced by mutual friends. He is also widowed and was absolutely ready for remarriage. I knew from the moment that Ed walked into my foyer that he was the man for me. Our stories were so similar. He had been happily married, as I had been, and he was eager for a family life. He did not want to date and to be single. I felt the same. Had I not had the first relationship and the dinner dates with various men, I might not have

> **A HARD ACT TO FOLLOW**
> *The widower may not relinquish memories/photos of the first wife*
> *You may feel constantly compared*
> *It may be difficult to blend with old friends, from both sides*
> *The children, yours and his, will vie for attention*
> *Balance is key to making the relationship succeed*

grown enough to appreciate what Ed offered. And I knew that it would be complicated because he has three children. They are in college but come home enough that our time alone together is precious and hard to put together.

"I have learned that a divorced man, even if he has kids, does not want the responsibilities that a widowed woman has. He doesn't want to take on her kids so totally and constantly. With Ed, there is none of this—he understands my story and I understand his. But we have other problems. Like the ghost of the first wife and the ghost of my first husband. Whatever Ed does, I admit I find myself comparing it to my former husband's style. I am sure that Ed feels the same about my actions. He probably asks himself how his wife would have done it. What can we do? This is our reality. But I know that he wants me, that we have only the present and the future."

Remarriages after widowhood are believed to have a better success rate than those that occur after divorce. Both partners have not failed at a relationship but have lost out. It is their determination and sense of commitment that puts them in a different place—they work very hard to make the new family a success. The innocence of youth has been replaced with responsibility and the realization that the world is less than fair, less than perfect. Often the widower is especially grateful to his new wife for entering his life and righting the wrong, filling the loneliness. However, this form of instant family man has similar obstacles to others who begin a second marriage with children.

According to Mimi, Ed was the perfect father for her children. "I could not believe how he treated my kids. They were so starved for male affection and for a father figure and he was willing, from he start, to pitch right in. I was fortunate that his children were grown and that our blended family primarily consisted of my kids and us.

That was plenty to handle. The adjustments, even when everyone has the best of intentions, is overwhelming."

The widower, as an instant family man, desires the same ingredients that a divorced man or professional bachelor desires once he decides it is time to settle down. These men seek a home, a family life, children to care for, monogamy and consistent sex and affection. The common belief which our society perpetuates is that men are commitment phobic and women are commitment starved. *The instant family man contradicts this theory. He is a man who wants stability and to leave the world of singlehood.*

In the case of Greta, her marriage to Wayne was a business proposition. Having met in the workplace, Greta confided to this man that she was recently divorced and attempting to raise her two small sons on her own. She worked full time and sent them to day care. Her fantasy that a man would save her had dimmed and she was in a panicked state. Wayne, surprisingly enough, was desirous of a marriage and appreciated the idea that Greta's sons were young enough to be malleable. Greta's ex-husband had moved half way across the country and was absent as a father. This allowed Wayne the opportunity he had been waiting for, to step in and become the instant family man. What Greta laments nine years later, at the age of forty-six, is the fact that she and Wayne were so preoccupied with their plan that they made no time for each other.

"I became pregnant with twins the first year of the marriage. While Wayne was delighted, I was distraught. I knew that he wanted children of his own, but I saw him as so absorbed with my sons that I assumed we'd take it from there." To his credit, Wayne has been an exemplary father, as he hoped to be, but Greta feels there is no enthusiasm for marriage. "I regret that I expected passion, because I've been so disappointed. I wanted a partner, not a savior. The truth is, the kids love him and the family life that Wayne envisioned does exist. I feel like it was never about me, but about what I could bring to the table."

For those women who crave romance and a whirlwind courtship, they will often find the instant family man to come up short. In a mature relationship which embodies true depth of caring and a meaningful connection, there may be romantic interludes and passionate moments, but the foundation is built of a stronger substance and is less ethereal in nature. The instant family man, be he a widower or a single man, has potential for such a balanced situation to be established. It is determined by what this man requires.

WHY THIS MAN?

If he is a dependent person and your actions do not address his needs, such as making him feel secure, he will become upset and difficult.

In a scenario with a widower, the future is determined by who the man is. If he is ready to fill the void, his partner will be frustrated, disappointed, and unable to do the job. However, if this man is someone who in mid-life realizes what he has achieved, in the workplace, in relationships with women and is now contemplating another experience, there is a good chance at success. He recognizes the important aspects of life and feels that the one area where he has been cheated is in having children and a home life. His extended family is dying and his own mortality faces him. The idea of being with a woman who is thirty in order to have babies might not appeal to him, yet the idea of meeting a woman who has a child, or several children already, is quite intriguing and suits his needs. He will absolutely embrace this opportunity, creating himself as an instant family man.

LOOKING FOR THAT MISSING PIECE

If this man makes plans for your perfect life together, he has already decided you are his missing piece. If you identify with the dream and it is a shared destiny, the pieces are in place. However, if you cringe and feel engulfed, the instant family man is not for you.

For Janice, the idea of an instant family man was foreign and unexpected. "Joe was in his late forties when I met him. I was divorced, with a little girl, Amanda, and working very hard to make ends meet and still take care of her. He was pretty happy-go-lucky. He had been married for a long time, but never had kids. He traveled a lot on his job, selling medical equipment, and had enough money to do whatever he wanted. He really had no intention of becoming serious with me. We met at a dinner party, and hit it off immediately. At first I always got a sitter for Amanda when Joe and I went out. When we saw we had the potential to make it as a couple, he began to come over to the house. He would arrive after work, and help with dinner."

Slowly over time, Joe became integrated into Janice and her daughter's lives. "Amanda craved a father, and he gave her just enough masculine attention. She was on a junior basketball team, and he practiced with her in the driveway. He even began coming to some of the games. He told me that he never expected to be doing any of this. My middle-class suburban type lifestyle was just not what he ever imagined. But he grew very attached to her. He had to rethink what he wanted in life. And unexpectedly, he decided he wanted us, our family to become his."

This unanticipated turn of events has worked out in everyone's favor. Joe was not a man who had any premeditated desire to become seriously involved in a relationship, let alone with a woman with a child. Joe recognized the responsibilities of taking on a wife and child at a time when he was responsible to no one but himself. The dividend for Joe is the richness of an instant family and the meaning it provided for him.

Women have been reporting that they are marrying men in their mid to late forties, who have never been married before. It appears that for many men, marriage and family have been delayed while they have focused on other aspects of their lives, such as career. A man whose goal is success, and has spent years in college, graduate school, and working his way up the ladder, may not have had the emotional energy to devote to a committed relationship. This man, a high achiever, could afford to make his life pleasurable in terms of creature comforts. Relationships may have been brief, lasting only as long as they did not interfere with his aims. Many of these men, as they approach fifty, realize that goals have been reached, but that they lack a fullness in their lives.

Lisa, a very attractive woman, accidentally became pregnant at age thirty-eight. She had an on-again, off-again relationship with a man that she was crazy about, but knew made her very unhappy. Although they lived together, and she had already had one miscarriage, he did not want to marry her and have their child. Therefore, she left the relationship to become a single parent. "I was making a good living and I was concerned that this was my last chance to have a baby. I dated during my pregnancy and the men did not even seem daunted. When my son, Jonathan, was eight months old, I met Ben. We seemed made for each other."

_____ Susan R. Shapiro and Michele Kasson, Ph.D.

Two years after they met, they married. Lisa felt that although they constituted a good couple, the motivation for Ben was timing. He was ready to settle down and become a family man. "I was sure that he fell in love with Jonathan before he fell in love with me. Jonathan was a perfect baby. Ben would throw him up in the air and carry him around on his shoulders. When we went out for the day, he wheeled the stroller. He showed Jonathan off to his family and friends. All of Ben's friends, approaching their mid-forties were getting married. Most of them had never been married before. Some were marrying divorced women with kids, so it didn't matter that Ben wasn't the biological father. It was the right time for Ben to have a family."

Jonathan was the ring bearer at the wedding. When Jonathan was four years old, Ben legally adopted Jonathan, and there was a party to celebrate. While there have been concerns over finances, schooling, and the typical issues which arise in any relationship, they have been able to work out their differences, and remain a stable, solid family.

For the woman who is mature and sometimes willing to forfeit excitement for stability, the instant family man makes sense. What she has to decipher is whether this man is at the right stage of life to accept a ready made family versus the man whose overriding inducement is to meet his dependency needs.

> **HOW TO SUCCEED**
> *Establish yourselves before the children are introduced*
> *Be sure of his motivations*
> *Learn his hopes for the future*
> *Let him know your expectations*

4

*"I would be married, but I'd have no wife,
I would be married to a single life."*
— Richard Croatia

COMMITMENT PHOBIC AND SERIALLY MONOGAMOUS

We all have met this man. He will reach the age of fifty and has been married two or three times. Or he has never been married but moves from one serious relationship to another. He cannot make promises. The relationship is always stormy with a beginning, middle and end. He is a charmer who cannot be alone for very long. Every relationship appears to be the special one. Jack Nicolson's memorable character in the film, *Carnal Knowledge* exemplifies this kind of man. He begins his long history with women in college, surrounded and admired by the opposite sex. Because he is unable to find the "perfect mate" he spends the rest of his days in emotionally fraught, unsuccessful liasons. By the end of the movie, he can only be moved by a prostitute.

These men desire a commitment even as they fear it.

Susan R. Shapiro and Michele Kasson, Ph.D.

They want both the connection and wish to escape the intimacy and demands of being connected. In Shakespeare's *Hamlet*, Hamlet wrestled with his feelings toward Ophelia to the point where she lost her mind. Although he claimed she was to be his wife, he suggested instead, "Get thee to a nunnery, go." Ophelia, confused and bereft by Hamlet's command, leaves the relationship, believing she has somehow wronged her partner. In her dire misery, she drowns herself. Little schooled was Ophelia of the commitment phobic man. The woman who is lured by this kind of man is fooled because he is genuinely interested in her and craves a closeness. Usually the relationship begins quickly with all of the wonderful feelings and hopes that this will evolve into a true love. The lovers are swept away. There is a certain tension due to the hurried quality of the time spent together. It is as if they cannot get enough of each other with the man leading the way. He wants to be inside your skin, your head, your body and soul, at once and forever. It is too good to be the real thing. The message from this man is, let's run off together into the sunset, as one heart, one mind.

If only these stories could indeed end this way. Unfortunately, in the case of the men out there, a large part of the population is afraid of making a commitment to a woman. It has nothing to do with love, chemistry, promises made, time shared—it is all about fantasy. The fantasy is perpetuated by the commitment phobic man and you become not only the object but the victim. The good things happen because this man seeks affirmation from you, representative of the opposite sex. He wants to be loved and he is genuinely sincere at the time. The connection becomes real, and the layers are unpeeled. The commitment phobic/serially monogamous man approaches the center, which is comprised of feelings of abandonment and engulfment. This mixture results in a strange and perplexing dance toward and away from us. Because he is so facile at being loving and involved, when he withdraws, we are devastated.

> The burn-out/commitment-phobic man *has trouble removing himself from his past. He tells you straight away of his inability to make a commitment based on his previous unhappiness. You do not really hear him. Then he resists yet persists, and you fall in love anyway.*

Theresa, who works in the fashion industry in Miami, has been dating Art, an entrepreneur, for the past eighteen months. Theresa has never been married and Art is divorced with two young children. On their first date, Art confided in Theresa that his ex-wife had cheated on him with her tennis instructor. Theresa was empathic and supportive as Art explained that he was in no frame of mind to remarry based on his history.

THE FLAVORS OF COMMITMENT PHOBICS

The Burn-Out. *He has been severely hurt in a past relationship and hasn't yet recovered*

The Pie in the Sky. *He's afraid of closing the door and risking the loss of someone better than you*

The Push and Pull. *He wants you but cringes when it is for real*

The Media Junkie. *He has been taught all of his life through TV sitcoms, radio, film and magazines, to run away from marriage*

"I was convinced that there was a mutual caring and we were very attracted to each other. I listened closely when he spoke about his son and daughter and about the trials and tribulations of being divorced and the custody arrangement. But mostly he was very angry at his ex-wife for having had an affair. It was almost as if he couldn't get over it. And he had been dating for the past three years, maniacally. I wasn't the first woman he had become involved with.

_____ Susan R. Shapiro and Michele Kasson, Ph.D.

We had a terrific time together. We both loved to water ski and go boating. We loved to go to movies. Still, there was a problem right from the start, he was always furious at women, no matter how many he dated, because of his unfaithful ex-wife. I knew that he would never settle down with me, although all the feelings were right. I tried everything because I really wanted him. Finally I walked away."

The pie in the sky/commitment-phobic man *is truly serially monogamous. He doesn't miss a beat as he glides from one relationship to the next with great finesse. He searches for the idealized woman who has yet to come along.*

At the age of forty, Tina has been with Brian for three years. Although she believes it to be a committed relationship, she doesn't believe that Brian will ever marry her. She is aware that he has had several relationships before theirs, and knows that he left each of them, having found fault with the woman. "I became pregnant after we were together for a year. I wanted to have the baby and thought it would be wonderful for my two children. I thought a baby would solidify the relationship, but I think that Brian is looking for a goddess to bear his child. In the end I had an abortion which I regret to this day. Brian is my age and never married. His lifestyle tells me that he never will marry. Although I know that I want to be married again, there is something about Brian that keeps me there. Sometimes when we are at a party or out at a restaurant, I see him looking around, almost assessing the crowd for his next partner. I have watched him flirt with women, in any and every situation. For some reason, I'm stuck on Brian. Maybe it's is sweetness, despite how tumultuous the relationship has been. He has actually begged on his hands and knees for me to come back when we've broken up."

All too frequently relationships end because of the

expectation that there is another person out there who is the better mate. Such is the case with Diane and Kevin. They had been together for four years when Diane realized that she wanted him to commit to her. She had just turned thirty-five and felt it was the right time to settle down. Divorced without children, she was tired of the single life and convinced that Kevin was the right partner for her. Kevin, the antithesis of her first husband, was outgoing and social. Together they made a splendid couple. When Diane approached Kevin on the subject of commitment, she met with amazing resistance. "His take on the relationship was a dream. He needed me to be his ideal woman. I was expected to change, depending on his needs. He doted on me and was totally in love with me. And although I asked for the commitment and loved his attention, I knew that I was slowly suffocating. Perhaps it ended for the best, but I was astonished when he turned me down for a lasting connection. Today Kevin is still not married and simply moves from one relationship to the next, knowing that no woman will ever measure up. His pattern repeats itself and I feel fortunate to have gone on with my life. Today I am remarried to a man who is perhaps less exciting, but solid, dependable, and there for me."

The push/pull commitment phobic man is uneasy with himself which is the core reason for his multiple relationships. He cannot discover a balance between his hope for intimacy and his fear of being close.

When Faith met Jerry, she was forty-one and divorced with two children. Jerry was four years younger and divorced with one child. Together they partied, spent time with their children, skied and traveled. The relationship was wonderful for the first six months. Suddenly one day, Jerry began to act differently. "I felt as if he was Dr. Jekyll

_____ Susan R. Shapiro and Michele Kasson, Ph.D.

and Mr. Hyde. He would be evasive and not call. Then he would tell me he had to work late. He did not disappoint me when it came to plans with the children, but when it was just for the two of us, he stopped being available. I was so hurt and I was also astonished. I really didn't know what it was about. The strangest thing was that Jerry knew so much about me. He knew that what mattered most was that I could count on him. I could not imagine what was going on. I was so upset that I confided to several friends who really disapproved of my relationship with Jerry. They saw it as hurtful and unfortunate. They recommended that I break away before things got worse. But I was unable to do it—I really could not. It was as if I was totally locked in. I was attached to Jerry on some level I can't even explain."

What Faith found so striking about Jerry was his ability to be intimate, to draw her in. As with many men who are commitment phobic, there was intensity about the relationship that made her think he was available. He appeared to desire the connection, the love, and the commitment. Then, when he had won over this woman, he began to pull away. The pattern is such that the commitment phobic man doesn't leave completely, instead he leaves in bits and pieces, so that the woman is left hanging. Eventually the commitment phobic man becomes critical of the object of his desire. Those very qualities which he once appreciated and admired are now at the center of his discontent.

"What happened with Jerry was that he gave me mixed messages for weeks. He pushed me away and when I told him it was over, he told me he couldn't live without me. I stopped hearing these words as a compliment and began to wonder if it had anything to do with me at all. Because our children had grown accustomed to being together, it was more difficult to let it go. There were so many tugs. I began to see the entire relationship as one big mess. I would spend my time at work day dreaming about the things he had said, the promises he had made, in those early days. And whoever that man was, the man who professed his love and devotion, I realized he was gone for good. He had been replaced with a stranger who gave me an incredibly difficult time."

The media junkie/commitment phobic man is a product of our culture. When he meets a woman, it has been ingrained in him that this woman wants to marry him and his walls are very high. He believes in the double standard, women see marriage as their goal and men see marriage as prison. However, this does not prohibit him from a constant menu of relationships.

Debbie met Allen at a bar in Kansas City. She was immediately taken by his appearance which was deliberate and appealing. He wore a long ponytail and cowboy boots and had a penchant for country western music. Debbie, a former model, home for Christmas, was so drawn to Allen that she transferred her job to remain with him. "My first mistake was becoming available to Allen who liked to play hard to get, and wanted me to be hard to get. He is a sweet, caring, generous person who is accustomed to attention and confused about settling down. Out of any man I have ever dated, and I have never been married, Allen is the one I would spend the rest of my life with, given the opportunity. His relationships have had a steady pattern—the women are always several years older and still beautiful, and he has stayed with each for years. I fit that bill perfectly—I am five years older than he, I have done modeling and TV commercials. This is right up Allen's alley. He was convinced that I wanted him and that I somehow wanted to absorb him entirely, as if I was nothing without him. It wasn't the case at all. Sometimes I had

_____ Susan R. Shapiro and Michele Kasson, Ph.D.

the feeling that he didn't see me as different from other women. He had been with so many women who had apparently wanted him totally. To listen to Allen it was as if he was a priceless commodity. He intimated that I was just another hungry woman he had to fend off."

From the start, Debbie realized that Allen was suggestible and tremendously influenced by his friends and their lifestyle. His home was a shrine to himself, complete with high tech toys and games. "I was never at ease in Allen's house because it was a bachelor's haven and there was no room for anyone else. In the beginning of the relationship we were so close that it didn't matter, but when he started to move away from me I couldn't stand to be in his place. It was almost as if I was an alien. Things got terrible for us and I don't know why. I tried to communicate, but I could not get through. We went through a very bad period. He began to sleep in his clothes, and I was very, very sad. We had always slept naked, and I didn't understand what was happening. I began to feel very alone, even with him. It was a terrible existence, and then we stopped seeing each other. After several months, two of his best friends got married. I think this had an effect on him. Slowly, he came back to me and for the first time I think there can be some hope for the future."

THE LIFESPAN OF THE LOVE AFFAIR

The first few months are ecstasy and you find yourself unable to get him out of your mind. The second stage is agony and you cannot get rid of the pain. The end is belabored, with lots of back and forth. The bitter finale may leave one wrung out and bereft.

The power play between those partners in a commitment phobic relationship is not easy to identify. While the commitment phobic man swears undying love to you, he makes you so miserable that you pull away. When you announce that you won't accept the relationship as it now exists, he tells you that you have destroyed any vestige of hope. You are pegged the bad guy while he is orchestrating the entire third act. Whatever was euphoric about the relationship is long gone. It is replaced with his perception of your behavior which makes you the wrong person for him. *The commitment phobic/serially monogamous man is onto the next relationship because it has a newness, it provides him with the chance to meet the right woman.* By now you have become less to this man, and must not only heal your wounds but must regain yourself.

The profile of the commitment phobic man is one who has enough money, is accustomed to spending it lavishly and has grown accustomed to the attention of women. He is in control, he seeks you out, wins you over, finds you irresistible, and then, when the relationship reaches the point where a commitment is a natural next step, he finds you quite flawed. Thus he tortures you and the relationship sours. For many commitment phobic/serially monogamous men, there is no reason to commit. Even as these men age and become pros beyond pros at it, there will always be a younger woman, a new breed of innocents, who fall for his game.

When Eileen met Jet she was

THE EVOLUTION OF THE COMMITMENT PHOBIC RELATIONSHIP

He needs you all the time and you happily respond

You feel pressured but choose to ignore the symptoms

It's all happening too fast

He ingratiates himself to your fantasy

He becomes part of your life

When the relationship is ready to move forward, he pulls away

Susan R. Shapiro and Michele Kasson, Ph.D.

convinced that he was the one for her. From the start they shared common interests; tennis, working, music and travel. Even their careers in the hotel business meshed. At the age of thirty-seven, Eileen was absolutely ready for a serious and promising relationship. And Jet, at the age of forty-five, expressed similar desires. "He was my entire life. We had everything we wanted. Total communication, fabulous sex, and we were conversational but also comfortable during silences. We could do anything together or nothing together. I knew that he had been engaged before and had broken it off. This did not bother me because I saw our relationship as unique and whatever had happened in the past was not pertinent. It was not the same kind of connection. Ours was heaven.

> **THE GRASS IS ALWAYS GREENER**
>
> *He is in constant search of the right partner*
> *While he's loving you, he's leaving you*
> *The sex is wonderful, but more physical than emotional*
> *The love is in place, but love alone is never enough*
> *You will be cheated of his presence by his perpetual search*

"Nothing about Jet's lack of ability to commit was obvious to me. In fact, I believed that he and I were in the same place. What was really going on was that I did all the work and he simply agreed or went along for the ride. He spoke of having children and even did volunteer work with impaired children. He was religious and believed in family. Everything seemed right. Then he asked me to move in with him and I said that I would do so only if we were engaged. That was when it ended. He refused to become engaged and told me that he had no intentions of marrying me. I was destroyed. I was heartsick. We had been together for two years, always with the implication that it would become a marriage. Instead he went on to the next love of his life."

Several years later, Eileen remains single, as does Jet. They have become close friends, but Eileen refuses to let the friendship become anything more after what had transpired. "I won't ever trust Jet again. I still admire his good qualities and know that I will always love him. But I won't allow myself to be suckered in again. I really learned my lesson. In retrospect I see that Jet is an opportunist. I wonder if I was a genuine love interest or an opportunity. Now that I have distance from the entire episode, I know that he is out for himself in his business and I honestly think it filtered over to his personal relationships. This is very discouraging to me. We do not share the same values."

Commitment phobic and serially monogamous men are a by-product of our times. As times have changed, so has the concept of commitment. In the past, commitment was a means of assuring both parties of fidelity and constant sex, a family and protection. Today, a man may sate many of his needs without a traditional partner. He has a cleaning woman, take out food, and children from his first marriage. Why does he need to repeat his mistake in marrying again? There is an enormous choice of women for him who will be happy to take the ride, hoping they will be the lucky one. He perpetuates the double standard

> **IS THIS YOUR MAN?**
>
> Does he alternate between admiring you and devaluing you?
>
> Is he moody, showing irritability or anxiety?
>
> Is he impulsive and potentially self damaging?
>
> Does he reveal to you that he is empty inside?
>
> Does he have a temper and intermittent displays of anger?
>
> Is he constantly blaming other people?
>
> Is he in fear that you will leave him?

that women are in search of commitment and men do not feel so inclined.

If your partner exhibits a group of these traits, you have chosen a man who might have difficulty in a long term relationship. Classic symptoms of the commitment phobic man are the following: your partner has a tremendous fear that you will leave him, the closer you become. In contrast, he also feels that you will overwhelm him and he will be smothered. Since he is unable to achieve a balance between these two sensibilities, he will give you mixed messages. While all people are in conflict, most are able to discover a balance and to achieve intimacy. It is the commitment phobic person who becomes lost in these feelings and cannot establish the balance, thus he is crippled. The commitment phobic man yearns to be connected even as he pushes it away. Because he is serially monogamous and the affection of a woman is so meaningful to him, he has become very skilled at winning your heart.

WARNING SIGNS

When you meet this man listen carefully to his story. How many women has he left? Has he broken engagements? How many women haven't measured up? If this man has been serially monogamous for more than five years, beware!

Women who have been in search of a mate are easily taken in by the commitment phobic man. He is quite polished at courting and enamoring you. He plays to your fantasies and has an excellent sense of your needs. The relationship moves at a quick pace. He desperately elicits your loving attention, but once he has achieved his goal, it makes him uneasy. To outsiders, it may appear as though you are a challenge and a conquest. However, his emotions are genuine, and this is the tricky part for the woman. She holds on to those feelings long after he becomes absent from the relationship.

There are several consistent issues which play into the minds of men and keep them from committing. Fear of responsibility to you, and possibly to your children, when so far he has only been responsible to himself, is a factor. In addition to this emotional fear is the real financial fear inherent in so many situations. He questions the guarantee that this relationship or marriage can prevail in the face of statistics. He questions whether you are truly the woman he was destined to meet and share the rest of his life. He has developed the habit of being alone. It is not easy to make room for someone else, even if he is desirous of it.

NAVIGATE YOUR PATH

You must begin to decipher the man who is injured but capable of healing and going forward with his life at last, versus the man who is unquestionably commitment phobic and offers no hope.

Francine, age forty-one, met Will, age forty-seven, two years after her marriage dissolved. There was an immediate attachment. "He liked me. He was sexy, romantic, and he even wanted to be with my kids. He would kiss me all the time in public places. He showed such joy at being with me, it was a treat."

Emotionally fragile when she met Will, Francine felt that it was her vulnerability which was the main attraction for him. She saw that he appreciated her best qualities, and was willing to be a part of her world. "Will loved hanging out with my kids. He was generous to them. He was interested and involved in a way that felt genuine. He was loving, romantic, and physically giving." Thinking back on the breakup, she felt that she had been used. "He

_____ Susan R. Shapiro and Michele Kasson, Ph.D.

> ## THE COMMITMENT PHOBIC'S M.O.
>
> *He is all over you after the second date*
>
> *Somehow he is under your skin—you can't get him out of your mind*
>
> *The description of past relationships has a familiar ring*
>
> *He admits that he is finally ready—you are the one—but his behaviors tell the truth*
>
> *You are told you are special and you believe it*
>
> *He has said it all before*
>
> *Holding back a commitment is his control over you*

wormed his way in. He was like a parasite, working himself into my life. He never wanted a commitment. He finds vulnerable women and once they believe him, want him, and need him, he disappears." Francine discovered that this was a pattern of Will's after speaking with a mutual friend. He was dating someone new with a similar situation to hers. Before Francine's time with Will, he was with another woman who had children. "This is his pattern. He doesn't want to be alone, but if you ever make noises that you want to strengthen your relationship, he's out the door. I knew at the end that he had begun to sleep with someone new, and had already left me. I wish I had listened at the beginning when he said that he didn't want any involvement."

When Ginger met Ken, he was with another woman at the health club. She watched him from afar and when the woman walked away, he approached her. "I should have known from the get go that he was trouble. How could he saunter over to me so easily after having been with someone? He would do it to me too. He told me that I was pretty and that this woman was only his friend. I never asked anything more. He was totally romantic, leaving love notes and sending flowers. He was sexy and handsome, honest and hardworking. He worked in construction and I was in sales. Our rhythm was

> **REASONS MEN COMMIT**
> *They are ready for companionship and a best friend*
> *There is a deep emotional attachment between you*
> *There is sexual fulfillment*
> *There is a sense of humor*
> *He is ready to make a change in his life*

steady and the relationship was progressing nicely. After nine months he asked me to marry him, but I had this sense that he didn't mean it. I don't know why. I suppose it was because the relationship had begun so quickly. Both of us were divorced. I had children and so did he. And while he was gentle with me, he was not gentle with his children. I began to wonder who this man really was.

"Then I met his cousin and he told me that Ken had been married five times and had children in various parts of the country. Apparently he would commit to these women and then decide he could not stay. The only difference between Ken and the men who will not commit is that he married his girlfriends and then decided to pull out. It was very strange. I was fortunate that I wasn't the sixth wife. And yet I had wonderful times with this man and had he been truthful, it might have worked. Once I stepped back it looked murky and wrong."

Casey, at the age of thirty-five, is a manicurist in a small town in the Mid West. She has been dating Mike, a building inspector, for the past two years. "He is kind and smart, when he allows himself to be. I don't think he's dated many women, and I don't think he's very good at it. I would pour out my heart and he used to listen to me. Now he says he's heard enough. I tell myself that if this relationship doesn't go somewhere I might as well leave. I can't, I'm hooked on him. It's like an obsession. Mike is always late, which hurts me and makes me feel like I don't count. He takes advantage of my good nature and I accept it. I'm always available for him and he can't be for me. I keep thinking that if we get married, I won't worry about him. Everything I say turns into an argument. He is critical of me. My friends and relatives tell me he's no good and that I should not be with him anymore. But I cannot let it go.

When we do not see each other, he's all over me. He calls and begs for me to come back. Then when we are back together, it starts all over again. I want a commitment and to have babies. He says that he wants babies too. But he won't promise anything. I see his good qualities, he would be a good and kind father. But he's very moody, so it's difficult. And he is set in his ways, like an old man. Sometimes I feel so good with him and other times we argue. We have broken up and gone back together many times. When he knows I've had it, and that I mean it, he comes to me. I am strongest when he's begging. But no matter what we fight about, he won't make the commitment. He likes to pursue and does not want me to pursue him. I plan to stick this out with Mike. I have a feeling that one day he'll make up his mind and stay for good."

A stellar example of a commitment phobic man who overcame his obstacles to marry and have children is Warren Beatty. When he married Annette Bening, the eyes of the world watch-ed in disbelief. As she gave birth to their children, Beatty offered hope to women everywhere that the commitment phobe can change his tune. We must remember that men require the love and affection of a significant other just as much as women do. In an honest, loving,

> **HOW TO GET HIM TO COMMIT**
>
> Put it on the line—take the risk of losing him
> Estimate the timing—feel him out
> Go into couples counseling
> Take time apart in order to appreciate time together
> Gently prod him if you are on solid ground

relationship commitment exists. It is not a command performance, but the basis of a meaningful relationship. It is no longer a question of a woman asking for something and a man refusing. Rather, the commitment develops naturally. It offers nourishment and safety in an ever changing world.

5

*"Lives like a drunken sailor on a mast,
Ready with every nod to tumble down."*
— Shakespeare

THE ADDICT

There are many kinds of addictions that afflict modern day men. Be it an addiction to alcohol, drugs, work, gambling, tobacco or women, the man who is addicted brings pain and suffering to those closest to him. As his partner, a woman finds herself competing with the addiction. Until this man makes the decision that you are more significant than his addiction, it is a no win situation. We have to question why women choose to live with such a man and what their requirements are, be it co-dependency or co-addiction, that they are able to stand it. Regardless of what the addiction is, it begins with a compulsion, an internal urgency for relief. The true addict cannot be without his addiction.

Ours is a society that tends to glamorize the addict, especially the alcoholic. Most notably, during prohibition, the idea of escaping to a speakeasy was considered the ultimate recreation. During the 1920s, F. Scott Fitzgerald made his literary debut, followed by his personal demise, due to his alcoholism. It is so much a part of the American culture, that *Guys and Dolls*, a Broadway smash success, reveres Sky Masterson, the macho gambler/drinker, notorious bad boy. When Masterson makes a play for the young, mousy woman who serves in the Salvation Army, he is really making a play for his soul. In the 1995 Mike Figgis film, *Leaving Las Vegas*, Nicolas Cage gives the academy award winning performance of an alchololic who is determined to drink himself to death. It is one of the more poignant, desperate and heartbreaking exposés of the world of the addict. In this film, the woman he loves cannot intervene to save him. She is aware of his impending destruction yet is immobilized.

There are those celebrities of our pop culture such as Andy Warhol, who condoned drugs and alcohol, idolizing them to another level. At the same time, the music icons of the sixties began their quick steady march toward drug addiction. Those rock musicians who come to mind are Jim Morrison of the Doors, Janis Joplin and Jimi Hendrix each of whom died of overdoses at the mercy of their addiction.

The most pressing problem for a woman who is involved with an addict is the lack of intimacy. While it appears on a good day that she and her lover are connected, when real issues surface for him, he will abandon her for his crutch, his addiction. *The Men Out There* emphasizes the need for women to establish healthy goals which are obtainable with their chosen partner. The aspiration of being with a man who is balanced enough to provide stability is the hope. In the case of the addict, the woman is up against an unwilling participant in this dance and her pain is acute.

Today, in place of the musicians of the sixties and seventies, our youth has the tales of their sports heroes to influence them. Only recently have we read of Dwight

Goodin's comeback after a major bout with drug abuse and the jeopardy of Darryl Strawberry's career due to chemical dependencies. And in politics, our nation's capital has a mayor, Marion Barry, who has been convicted of drug possession. With the public eye on these figures, one questions the effect of such role models on our future generations. And of course, in terms of the men out there, there is the continual seduction of these accepted behaviors.

IS HE OR ISN'T HE?

The addict is an alluring manipulator. The woman who is initially drawn into his life will be unassuming and unable to decipher the clues. He wants to keep her in the dark about his addiction—and will succeed for a period of time. Eventually he will reveal himself unwittingly or she will catch on.

When Rachel first encountered Jeremy at a Starbucks in New York City, she was impressed and touched by his story. He explained that he was getting divorced and in danger of losing joint custody of his small sons because his wife contended that he had a drug and alcohol addiction. "I was so sorry to hear what he was going through. I thought that he was a recovered alcoholic and had not touched drugs for a long time. I knew the pain of not being with your children. And as a twice divorced and single mother, I wanted to help this man. That was the beginning of the problem, that I actually was taken in. Jeremy was a stand up comedian who was hired for parties and each night after he finished his gig, he would come to my place. He never asked for a drink at first, and then after a while, he would have some wine. I saw a marked difference in his personality. And I began to suspect that he did drugs as well. I learned after seven long months of erratic behavior that he was an addict, and that he had given up nothing. He did cocaine and he drank liquor. By the time we split, I was heartbroken. I thought that he was a terrific guy and I was very tight with him. I think that aside from the addictions, he was the closest to perfection of any man I'd ever dated."

As in the case of Rachel, many women discover that the addict is the man of their dreams. He is sympathetic, caring, loving and wants very much to be connected to a partner. Unfortunately, the addiction is what prohibits true closeness. There can be no intimacy in a relationship with a man who has an addiction. For the woman who falls in love with a man who is an addict, she is fighting another sort of mistress. In this drama, there is not the ever present demanding ex-wife nor is there another lover and an unhappy triangle as a result. Instead there is the constant draw of the addiction itself.

The addict has deep seated insecurities and for a long period of time has run to his vice rather than face these insecurities head on. A woman often believes herself to be the savior and that she can make the difference. His issues may involve anxiety, self-esteem, and rage, which are common problems and concerns of other men. For most men, these issues are internalized, while for the addict, they become obvious. A woman who sits across the table from a man who is an alcoholic has visible, concrete representation of his troubles. She thinks that the problem is substance abuse, but in fact, the factors are not so simple. This man has found an outlet, but cannot be so quickly cured as she may naively believe.

> **THE CORE OF AN ADDICTION**
> *He is preoccupied with his addiction*
> *He will always deny the addiction to you*
> *It dominates his thoughts and way of life*
> *You are excluded without fail*
> *None of what he does is deliberately cruel to you*
> *He loses sight of what is beneficial to him*

Penny, at the age of forty-one, has been divorced for several

Susan R. Shapiro and Michele Kasson, Ph.D.

years and has dated extensively. The most meaningful relationship of all transpired with George, who was an electrician in a nearby town in Nebraska. "I noticed George at a bar where I went

> **THE STEPS TO DISCOVERY**
>
> You rationalize your partners actions
> You deny that anything is wrong
> You begin to notice inconsistent behavior
> You decide you are the savior—your love can make the difference
> Too late you get the picture, you become disappointed/angry

during lunchtime three years ago. I never go to bars, but I was recovering from cancer and had recently had my last dose of chemotherapy. I was celebrating quietly, sitting alone, and he was there with a friend. He came over to me and did not comment on the fact that my hair was only an inch long. I was attracted to his humanity. We connected at once and began to date exclusively. I fell madly in love with him. I'd say that within two weeks time, I had suspicions that he was an alcoholic."

Penny noticed that George always needed a drink. It confused her that he did not fit the profile of an alcoholic. He was successful in his own business, hard working, and took care of Penny financially. He was punctual and respectful of her. He was not abusive or physically careless. His honesty was appreciated by Penny and she truly felt that he was there for her. "He drank so steadily that it frightened me. There was not one time I can recall where he did not have a drink. It's almost as if it didn't effect me directly but was continually present. I felt very safe with him but had this underlying sense of something wrong because I knew he drank. If he had not been an alcoholic, I would have married him and been with him for the long haul. For ten months of the time we were together, I tried to persuade him to seek help and to stop drinking. I kept thinking that I could make it happen. When he was sober

I begged him to do something. I suspect that his ex-wife was an alcoholic as well. I adored him and I asked him to come with me when I was relocated for work. I thought that he could dry out then, in another part of the country. He refused. Finally I realized I could not change him and I knew in my heart of hearts that an addict is an addict. He did not want to be cured and that was the end for me. Today I believe he has found a partner who also drinks. This makes me very sad."

Our society is prone to addiction. It is not specific to men or to adults, nor is it specific to alcohol or to drug abuse. However, it does often manifest in these two manners. *What we are addicted to is far reaching and the implications color all of our lives.* We have issues with food, sex, youth, materialism, exercise, power, caffeine, media, tobacco, prescription drugs, and a multitude of other hooks, as well as the obvious offenders which are alcohol and drugs. While this chapter concentrates on the male addict in midlife, it is important to remember how much of a social consideration addiction is. Dependence is not the same as abuse. Abuse implies the loss of ability to function at work and at home, the potential for hazards and legalities, such as arrest for disorderly conduct.

An addict will need increased amounts of the substance because with time he will gain a tolerance for it. There will also be withdrawal symptoms in the absence of the substance. This person's life revolves around activities that enable him to use the drug or alcohol. His life is dictated by this dependence and certain interests are curtailed or encouraged as a result. Furthermore, use may continue even if the person is aware that it is not to his advantage but to his detriment.

Susan R. Shapiro and Michele Kasson, Ph.D.
THE TELL TALE SIGNS OF THE ADDICT

It is not the frequency with which this person needs his substance but how it effects him that determines the addicted personality. At a party he will drink excessively and awaken the following morning in a funk. The funk will dissipate only once he has had another drink. Other people do not partake on a daily basis—the need is in response to external events. This abuser may binge only on occasion but has a definite pattern.

Although there are many kinds of addictions, the women interviewed for this chapter were primarily concerned with a partner's alcoholism or drug abuse. Victoria's story exemplifies the futility of these relationships if professional help is not sought. When she met Hank she was legally separated and the mother of two teenage children. Hank, at thirty-five, was six years her junior and divorced without children. He lived with his sister and practiced dentistry in a building several blocks away from his home. He was practically engaged, but upon meeting Victoria, decided he could not allow this opportunity to pass him by.

"At first I was thrilled with his attention. After a while, I suspected that he was obsessed with me and it was unhealthy. However, my marriage had been so unhappy and dry that I craved an overwhelming desire and attention from a man. He called constantly and had to know where I was. In between patients, he would sneak out and meet me for coffee. He sent me notes and gifts and we would be together almost every night. My kids were suffering and my performance at work as a chef was suffering, but I became as obsessed as he did. Then I noticed that he wasn't only obsessed with me, but he was obsessed with drinking. And he would change from the sweet, kind, devoted man who would look into my eyes into this monster, control freak who would lose his temper and become violent, belligerent and combative at the drop of a hat.

"I was scared to death. He would call my friends at two in the morning, instead of calling me. After six months of good and bad times, I knew I had to put an end to it. The very suggestion that he get professional help sent him into a tizzy. He believed because he was a dentist that he was immune. I think this was very dangerous for his patients and for his own life. When I told him I no longer wanted to be involved he went berserk. He came to my house in a drunken rage and screamed outside my window until I let him in. I almost called the police. I knew that I could never be with this man after that. It wasn't about me, it was about his drinking and his obsession with me."

Despite how flattering Hank's initial attention was to Victoria, once she recognized the depth of his addiction to both her and to alcohol, she extricated herself completely. Yet in many scenarios, women find themselves repeating their pattern and going from one addicted man to the next. It is almost as if they enter a room filled with people and are immediately drawn to the person who is poison for their soul.

CO-DEPENDENT OR NOT?

Do not be fooled by the trend that women are labeled co-dependent. Historically, this term arose as the buzz word for couples who were involved with alcohol. Women were seen as the enablers for their men. Instead they may be viewed as survivors.

Jeanne, who lives in New Hampshire and is a case manager at a hospital, is representative of what some call co-dependent. The two most serious relationships in her life have been men who are addicts. "I was with a man for seven years who I married because he promised he had come clean. He went into rehabilitation and was sober for over a year. It was then that he convinced me to marry him. After he returned to his addictions, crack and alcohol, it became a living hell. I was wiped out financially and emotionally drained by his ways. He is exactly my age but from such another background. I often think that it was his years in Vietnam that caused this to happen to him. I thought that he loved me more than anyone and that love was enough. I learned the hard way that he wasn't only dependent on me, but on his habits. I nurtured him and I was a great co-dependent person because I could help him. I decided that he was my best friend on earth and that he needed me. It was strange how when he was clean he could make money and how when he wasn't we were both absolutely broke from his addiction. I was a middle-class girl with middle-class values and had worked for my college education. I was told that if I worked hard and did the right thing that life would be good. I was not prepared for the secret hell of life with this man. I knew that there was no choice after I had tried everything and so we divorced."

Within a year, Jeanne had relocated and found a new job and was hoping for a fresh start. The first man who she met after the divorce pursued her relentlessly. "I knew he was not right for me and I could sense that he was another addict but I began to date him anyway. He drank a lot of scotch and beer and I saw many of my ex-husband's tendencies in this man. I knew it was temporary and that I could not become committed again to someone like that. Still, the fact that I dated him at all is worrisome to me. I stopped seeing him because after chasing me relentlessly, he became preoccupied with another woman. This woman moved into the empty room in his house and she was also a drinker. I fell by the wayside. He never asked me how I felt about her presence and I found that to be a betrayal.

He was a troubled guy who knew how to camouflage it. This time I left before I got in too deep."

Currently there is a great deal of research conducted on the biological predisposition to addiction. It has been found that sons of alcoholic fathers frequently become alcoholics themselves. This appears to be due to biological markers in their genetic makeup. For the women who fall in love with these men, the addict offers highs and lows, and an eventual breakdown in the relationship. While in the throes of the affair, the addict, prone to anxiety, may turn to alcohol as a way to assuage his upset. It is a form of anesthetizing himself. The angriest of men, those who become violent, may tend to be more susceptible to cocaine or to heroine addiction. Along with both alcohol addiction and drug addiction is the obsession with one's partner. The tremendous expectation is that she will provide a port in any storm.

Sandra's live-in arrangement with Howard has been influenced by his bouts of alcoholism since the beginning. While she has remained at his side, she has also grown tired of covering up for him and being his partner in this dark secret. To the outside world Sandra and Howard lead the good life. Their home is magnificent and their children

---

WHO IS ADDICTED TO THE RELATIONSHIP?

Will you do anything to be in this relationship?
Do you have porous boundaries?
Is his pain your pain?
Are you always worried what other people think of you?
Are you always saying you're sorry?

WHO FINDS THE ADDICT?

Women who have been abused
Women with a poor sense of self
Women who require the relationship to be all encompassing

Susan R. Shapiro and Michele Kasson, Ph.D.

> **SPOTTING THE MALE ADDICT**
> *Does he confide that his father was an addict?*
> *Does he self-medicate at the drop of a hat?*
> *Does he drink at inopportune times?*
> *Does he have several drinks before the night out?*
> *Does he have blackouts?*

from their previous marriages are delightful. But for Sandra, the stakes have grown exceedingly high and she wrestles with the conflict of leaving Howard. "I know how much he needs me but I dread the days that he has been drinking. I feel that he isn't the same person and I can't escape his wrath. Howard is a wonderful man, community minded, involved in school politics. But when he drinks he is critical and cruel. I would call him a mean drunk. Recently we were out with another couple and the food was not served on time. Howard lost his mind. He stood up and threatened to turn over the table. I was mortified. I ended up placating him. This is the story of my life. I never know when he will drink, but I know what will happen when he does. The next day he had a bracelet and roses delivered to my office. What I know is that I should never leave Howard. He and our collective children depend on me."

In Sandra's case, there has never been a physical encounter with Howard, but a threat of one. Other women are not as fortunate as she. There are numerous tales of women who remain with their addict with full knowledge of hovering physical abuse. A battered women syndrome does not necessarily fit into the story of the addict, but women do become victims of men who abuse substances. Mallory's situation is not as benign as Sandra's. Having been involved with a heavy drinker for the last eight months, she has recently left the relationship.

"Kurt is a typical bad boy with loads of anger. He is angry at his ex-wife, his ex-boss, his dysfunctional kids, and at me for being a happy person. I cared for him very much and I wanted to bring this to a marital close, but when I investigated all parts of the puzzle, I realized it was not a healthy place for me to be, and that it had to end. Because of his addiction, he could not offer a full life. The drugs always got in the way. It was a frightening experience. I feared for my life. The physical violence was out of control. I knew the sickening feelings that came along with it all too well from my ex-husband. This man was nice when sober, and strangely quiet. It was the violence that pushed me away ultimately. After my past with men who do drugs or drink, I could see the writing on the wall. This time I left within months, not years. I wasn't about to be hit again."

Marcia, at forty-four, has been twice divorced and single for the last eight years. In the past year she has been able to walk away from a dire co-dependent relationship which lasted for three years. Marcia, as a stunt artist in Southern California, found that her relationship with Barry actually caused her to lose a few important jobs. In time, she began to lose herself. "Barry was the most intense love relationship of my life. He had an alcohol and drug abuse problem which required me to become co-dependent in order to be his partner. I thought I could make a difference in those days. I thought I was a savior. Today I have taken any co-dependent need I have and transferred it to my work. While I am not sated romantically since I have left Barry, at least I can sleep at night again.

TRIUMPH OVER DESTRUCTIVE RELATIONSHIPS

Accept that you are looking for love

Decide what kind of mate will satisfy your desires

Do not repeat your mistakes

You are worthy of a man who doesn't abuse substances

An addict is not available for a real connection

_____ Susan R. Shapiro and Michele Kasson, Ph.D.

Being single in California, I can't afford to let another addicted relationship get in the way, either emotionally or monetarily. I'm ashamed to say that I spent several years of my life worrying if this man was coming home or not. This component of not knowing kept us from having any complacency. There was always this element of chance. It was exciting and it was heartbreaking. I think that he was drawn to abuse to fill the hole in his life, and I was drawn to him to fill the hole in mine. I began to realize that I was living my life for him and not for myself. I was struggling to support a man who could barely keep his head above water. At first I got angry at myself and then the domestic abuse began. We had become angry at each other.

"Barry was a cocaine addict and an alcoholic. This was the worst combination. He was very volatile. We lived together and twice I moved out and then moved back in. When I look back on it, I cannot believe I lived this life. Because he was a rock and roller, a drummer, we were out at parties all of the time. Our private life was a roller coaster ride without any peace. I was unhappy all the time. I never felt like I could breathe. He definitely loved me in some twisted way, and the sex was great. I would tease him and make him jealous, and he would go crazy and want me all the more.

RE-EVALUATING THE WOMAN'S ROLE

It is difficult to make changes in a long term relationship. Initially we may deny the problem which exists. We cover up for him in social situations, and lie to his boss. The addict's predominant need is for us to protect him, but one cannot deny the emotional bond. When the man is addicted, it is frequently the woman who takes the initiative on the path to recovery.

"My ego needed the other men because he made me

feel incompetent. I could not get it right. Always he gave me a hard time, and it became demoralizing. I knew it was about his addiction, that he put me down because he did not feel good about himself. I knew that I was competent and that I could get it right. It killed Barry to see me succeed in any area except my work. I think he was supportive of my work because he wanted to be with the "right" person. He had selfish motives. Although he was not a good person for me, I knew that he was creative, so I stayed with him. I kept believing I could make him better. I tried and tried to convince him to get cured, but he had no desire. He told me that, "You could sleep when you're dead." My entire life was going down the drain. I needed money to leave and had none. At my urging, Barry's brother intervened. For a long time afterward I was scarred, and could not be with another man. Imagine that the first man I met out of this horror story was another addict, an alcoholic drug abuser. The same scenario was lining up for me. I already knew that he could not be there for me, and I broke it off. I knew it was like being on a tightrope without a net. It was all about him, all about his addiction. That is the nature of the beast."

For the duration of her marriage, Melanie chose to excuse and overlook her husband's bouts with alcoholism. Although he resisted seeking treatment, there was one incident that altered his manner of operating. No matter how often Melanie begged Ron to stop his drinking, it was to no avail. Only when he was away on business and arrested for lewd conduct in a bar, did the impact of his addiction become real to him. At first, Ron chose not to disclose the event to his wife, but to seek counseling.

"For ten years I begged Ron to stop drinking, especially when we were with the children and he was driving, which frightened me to death. There were days in my marriage that were so dreadful that I really wondered if I could stay. I never knew if he would return from work on time, or would be spending the evening in a bar. Too much of my life was dedicated to thinking about where Ron was and what

> **A DAY IN THE LIFE**
>
> *When children are involved your heart is in your mouth*
>
> *He puts you on edge, there is no way to determine his sobriety*
>
> *In his absence, you do not trust him*
>
> *The world you share is precariously balanced by his behavior*
>
> *A great deal of your life is spent covering for him*

he was doing. His moods were vile or if he was inebriated, he was falsely euphoric. I was frightened much of the time and I felt lost, as if I could not confide in anyone. Had this awful thing not happened when he was in Houston, I doubt that we would still be married. I was about ready to call it quits when he came to his senses and sought help. Today our family is intact and I am no longer living a lie. Had anyone told me this was possible four years ago, I would not have believed them. We do avoid certain people and certain places and our lifestyle has been affected, but in the long run, it's a small price to pay to have a husband who is no longer drinking."

Because of the complexity of addiction, there is no one simple solution for any of the men out there. For the woman who loves this man, there is the hope and desire for him to recover. Be it a marriage or a new relationship, the odds of success are contingent upon this man being able to break his habit. Denial of the addiction coupled with a society which condones it, makes it an arduous task. However, there are women who reap the rewards of a recovered partner.

Teddy was a man who had been unable to face his addiction to drugs and alcohol for many years. Once separated from his second wife, Maria, he realized that the custody of his children was dependent on his behavior. Maria, having pleaded with him to stop his addiction, signed an affidavit stating that her husband was a substance abuser and had a violent streak. "Whether Teddy and I remained married or not, I knew that his addiction to drugs and to alcohol was hitting all parts of his life. Even his career as a big time president of a company was beginning to unravel. I knew that the children did not need to be with a man who was not reliable. I like to think that if we do not divorce, he will pull his life together. If we do divorce, I still have the same hope. It is not only for my benefit, or for the benefit of the children, but ironically I continue to care for him as a person. And for his next partner, I cringe to think that she would have to go through what I have tolerated. I know that the next man I find will be as clean as a whistle. I cannot live like this any more. I have a strange feeling that Teddy is ready now to make a difference in his life. It really is his decision."

FOR THE MEN OUT THERE WHO SOLICIT HELP

A cornerstone of treatment in this country has been through self help groups such as Alcoholics Anonymous. Twelve step programs have been instrumental in changing the lives of many people. Currently there are other treatments for the addicted person which are available in most communities. Once he obtains help, the addict becomes free to pursue a meaningful, balanced relationship with his partner.

Samantha's story is unusual in that when she met Phillip he was a recovered alcoholic. Having been through a twelve step program, Phillip did not share the information with Samantha. She noticed he did not drink at dinner and declined even a glass of wine. Certain evenings he was unavailable for a few hours and while he explained these were business engagements, Samantha began to suspect that he was involved in AA. Phillip, at the age of fifty, was getting past a heart wrenching divorce, and was truly a kind and loving man who had endured pain.

"I saw that Phillip struggled to trust me and to let me in. I was patient because I knew instinctively that he was worth it. I was very taken with him and it was the kind of relationship I dreamed of. Having never been married, I was ready to be with a man who treated me compassionately. Our sex was a measure of the depth of our feelings for each other. But I always had this sense that Phillip was hiding something.

> **WHAT IS REQUIRED TO WIN**
> Look for all of the warning signs
> Do not neglect yourself for his needs
> Decide early on if he will seek treatment
> Be supportive but do not encourage the addiction

In the past few months he has confided in me. I was surprised at first, because although I was suspicious, I wasn't prepared for what he told me concerning his ex-wife. Apparently they were very close and had wonderful times together, and had been married for years. But alcohol had taken over their lives and had destroyed the core of the marriage. It was with great strength that he decided to join AA. His ex-wife refused to give up the drinking and that was why they had divorced. Several years after their divorce, he cared enough to try once more. They met at a mutual friend's home. Phillip listened to her slurred speech and observed her loss of motor control. He told me afterward that he knew he could never live with her again. I have no fears that he will return to his former ways. Although there is still great pain for Philip based on his history, we take it day by day."

Part II

The Lost Boys

6

"I know of no country, indeed, where the love of money has taken stronger hold on the affections of men..."
— Alexis De Touqueville

MONEY AND POWER

For the man who is about money and power, there is a sense of entitlement and superiority that other men do not flaunt. Their monetary success provides them with toys and an image to hide behind. For so many, these objects cover up their inner fears. Deep down they yearn for love and affection even as they are too immature to receive it. If you hope for a relationship with this man, you must see beyond his toys and show him the path to his feelings.

The competitive games that little boys play teach them the value of competition as adults in the workplace. As girls we are attracted to the athlete. As women our attraction has been translated to the man who produces money, the only currency we are taught to trade in. Thus, money becomes power. The goal is to win, and as Malcolm Forbes said, "He who dies with the most toys wins." Although we have heard the concept a million times, we reiterate that power is the capacity to earn status through possessions.

The man who makes a great deal of money receives respect and acknowledgement from both genders of all ages. In our society, men have traditionally been considered the breadwinners. Despite how far women have come, and what positions they have achieved in the workplace, men are more measured by their wealth and power than women. As Andrea, a litigator, explained her experience with the men out there, "During the day, when I'm in court, I deal with men constantly, and we are equals. But when we date at night, I'm again the fragile female and this man wields his weight, which is considered and valued by the amount of money he's made and how visible he is."

Many women struggle with the balance between home and career, and few choose to forgo marriage and children. Unlike men, their entire identity is usually not bound to their profession. In contrast, men with money and power have the option to have it all, but mostly what they have is only on the surface. The commitment this man makes is to his appearance to others. If he wishes to flaunt a family, his money can buy him one. It is the rare individual who can make the commitment to the family, achieving the relatedness and intimacy necessary for a complete home life, while continuing to focus on the presentation of his worth to others.

THE IRONY

Men who have been applauded and respected solely for their worth, who are spoken of in terms of the very power they have sought, wonder how any woman can want them for their heart and soul. After all, they are the commodity they have self-created.

_____ Susan R. Shapiro and Michele Kasson, Ph.D.

The paradox is that the male must be successful in order to become attractive to the female. Yet the means for achieving success may be the very ingredients which many women frown upon when encountered in a relationship. Generally, in our culture, if a man is not successful, then it is difficult for him to maintain his self-esteem. Certainly, with the loss of ego based on his lack of success, he may feel a loser in love as well.

Meg was divorced for one year from a very successful man when she met Russell at a dinner party. They took to one another immediately, and Meg's friends commented on what a great couple they would make. Russell called Meg a few times. The conversations suggested that this was a relationship in the making, but they never went out on a date. Russell stopped calling, and Meg chalked it up to another man who "talked the talk, but could not walk the walk." One year later, Meg was invited to another party given by the same friends "I hesitated before accepting, thinking that Russell might be there. I saw no reason to position myself that way. Then I decided that it wasn't significant. I wasn't dating anyone special then, and I thought I would see what would happen. Sure enough, he was there. And this time he asked me out at the end of the evening. When we went out, two nights later, he explained that he hadn't called me because he had been out of work. I think that his self-esteem was so tied up with his career that until he was back on his feet, he couldn't be involved with anyone."

Meg learned that Russell had established himself, and was on the fast track that meant so much to him. He had found the balance of emotional and financial power. "Russell feels good about himself, is making the kind of money that counts, and that is the measure for him. We are now able to have a relationship. I understand what it takes for him to be happy. Russell needed to feel successful in his career before he was available to love me. When he lost his job he thought of himself as a total failure and that he would fail with me too."

Another scenario is for power to meet power. We have observed couples in the limelight who have chosen partners who also appear to have power in their own right. For example, Ted Turner and Jane Fonda, Bruce Willis and Demi Moore, Tommy Mattola and Maria Carey all exhibit this trend. In the entertainment world, stardom demands a certain kind of partner. The power partnerships of Hollywood include Tom Cruise and Nicole Kidman, and of yesteryear, Liz Taylor and Richard Burton.

The most notable public figure of all is a real prince. Prince Charles' decision to marry Diana Spencer was premeditated and scrutinized. The fiction that as a prince and princess, he the powerful, she the fortunate recipient, on every level, could not prevail. Even with the best intentions, Charles' love for another woman was destined to destroy his marriage. As in the case with many money and power men, Charles ultimately had to have his way and those in his path suffered. Without knowing the particulars of these relationships, one can only speculate that when both partners are of independent means, it becomes more difficult for one to overcome the other. In other instances, the money and power man will purposely decide upon a partner who is not at center stage because he has another need altogether, to be the only star.

MONEY, POWER AND YOU

What we need to bear in mind is that one doesn't have to be wealthy and powerful in the real world in order to be a "money and power" guy. The issue is not how much he has, but what effect it has on his personality. Further, one must be concerned about how his attitude toward his money affects you. Interpersonal power is the issue.

Jacqueline's long term partner, Nick, worked at an after school center for inner city teenagers. His job involved fund raising, parent groups, and providing aid and guidance for difficult boys. Jacqueline, a receptionist at a gynecologist's office also worked hard, but did not receive the kind of attention that Nick did. "When Nick got a raise and additional responsibility at the center, he became impossible. I was very sorry to see it go to his head. When he started working there he had not invested his ego. By the end, if he had gotten ten more dollars a week he would have seen it as more power to him. I could not stand his attitude. He wasn't God. I also helped people at my job."

EGOCENTRICITIES

Positions of authority make it difficult for the woman who is not seen by her mate as an equal. She struggles to get his attention, in any way that she can. His inability to notice is significant. The money and power guy feels the world revolves around him.

Blythe's encounter with a money and power guy resulted in a short term unhappy marriage. At the age of thirty-seven, she believed her instincts to be on target. Scott, her husband, was an extremely successful entrepreneur who swept her off her feet. "I had been in therapy and thought I was on the road to self discovery. Although I noticed that Scott needed to have things his way, he was so charismatic and such fun. He was absolutely thrilling to me. And I admired how much time he put into his businesses because I really wanted the life it provided. I didn't know until we were actually married how insecure he was underneath and how demanding he became toward me. He had to show me how much better he was than I. And he became emotionally abusive. He had all of the rights in the family, he made all of the decisions because he had all of the money. He also had a huge amount of anger and was accustomed to using his money to get his way with people. What I learned about myself was that the money and power didn't do it for me. I wanted a husband and a family. I wanted a best friend, and not another fancy car or a necklace."

When Blythe left the marriage, she noticed that nothing about Scott's life was altered by her absence. In fact, as in the case with many money and power men, he simply marched forward, without varying his step, untouched by his divorce. "Within a few weeks time, I heard that he was dating several women. I'm sure that each had the fantasy of obtaining the big house and the status that he could provide. But what about the rest? What about his heart? I know how desperately in love with him I was and how unable he was to return that love. When I speak with him now, I still feel the tug, then I remember that I was one of those who fell for it. He could never really give me what I want. The world he has constructed for himself keeps him apart from any true feelings—which is what now counts in my world."

> ## WHAT MAKES HIM TICK?
> *He is the Wizard of Oz, hiding behind the curtain*
> *To the outside world he is extraordinary*
> *If he comes from poverty, he needs to prove himself*
> *If he comes from wealth, he needs to prove himself*
> *His money is his security blanket*
> *His attention is sought mistakenly, as if money makes him wise*

Susan R. Shapiro and Michele Kasson, Ph.D.
WHAT DOES MONEY HAVE TO DO WITH LOVE?

You are impressed with his lifestyle—he dazzles you and it feels like love. There is a magical, mystical quality—he is a whirling dervish, he makes things happen. If you look closely, you will notice your position in the hierarchy—you can never remain first in the money and power man's life for long.

Although this man may not intentionally hide behind his lifestyle and his toys, his possessions are a way of building his ego, and thus necessary for him in order to relate to a woman. This strategy goes awry when he has spent so much of his energy concentrating on his subsequent power that he hasn't developed the interpersonal skills and the emotional wherewithal to relate to anyone in a meaningful way. All too often his children are there to support his ego, rather than the other way around. Their accolades are his accolades. As he deals with a romantic relationship, he deals with his children. It is blurred and stymied by the armor that he wears. It is extremely important for this man to think of himself as an exemplary father, for his children are more of his possessions, and he prides himself on being able to take care of what is his. Even if there is a lack of true emotional involvement with his children, he is assured

HOW TO SPOT HIM
He has accumulated many toys, such as cars, planes, boats, and houses

He works hard and plays hard

He is critical of others because he is the best

There is a gradual belittlement of your achievements

He rushes to love you and disappoints you later

His needs must be met —and they are

He has gone through numerous relationships with women

that he will not be alone based upon the strength of the biological tie.

As his partner, you may relish the highs and tend to ignore the lows. When he is callow and lacking in intimacy, you will remind yourself of the good points. A money and power guy has a lot going for him—he is in charge in any setting. His opinion seems to have more weight than others', he is treated like royalty, and his world is insulated from the daily grind. Even if he feigns modesty, it is all about appearance.

Elle, at the age of thirty-six, found herself divorced from a money and power man. Living in a suburb in the Midwest, holding down a part time job, she dated several men and mothered her two children before meeting Michael. "I thought that because I knew his type that it could work out. He was recently divorced, and a prominent person in our community. He was so accustomed to people falling all over him. And I was supposed to be impressed. The truth was, I knew men like Michael because of my ex-husband. There were no surprises. There was nothing that Michael was showing me that I hadn't seen already. And I was cynical, because it hadn't worked out for me. But his demeanor and his physical appearance were so different than my ex-husband's that I began to believe in him.

"In retrospect, I think that I needed a loving partner and I made him that. I decided to ignore what made him tick — and the irony was that I understood his type all too well. He was another man who was always in charge, his money made people jump for him. If I had done everything he wanted, his way, I would have ended up married to him. Thank God I had some self-preserving instinct that stopped me.

"I think my eyes opened when it came to the issue of

children. It was easier for me to see him in relation to his kids than in relation to me. He wanted to forget about his fathering. He claimed that his kids were grown already. I thought they required his love and attention, but his view was that they were off in college and his energy was no longer necessary. This discouraged me. It was not a business deal, but his children we were talking about. There is no end to parenting, at any stage. Once I was really offered the choice to be with Michael or not, I realized that I did not want to uproot my own children and lead the life he expected of me. I really did love him but he became so difficult after a while."

What was particularly demanding for Elle was the fact that Michael resented the time she gave to her own children. "I was constantly torn and conflicted. I began to see that this is no way to live. Michael, because of all his power at work, and all his material goods, thought that he could make me an offer I couldn't refuse. The problem with Michael was that he was so accustomed to bossing people around every day in the office, that he couldn't believe that I didn't dance for him. He found this both appealing and unacceptable. I knew that I couldn't give him what he wanted and I became tired of trying. Later I heard that he remarried a woman with no kids. I hope that will work for him. We were together for two years. Finally I saw him as cruel and spoiled but that was not what he presented to the outside world. To the outside world he is a winner."

What is notable about Elle's story is that she was unfazed by her partner's money and power. It seems that her money and power man found fault with her priorities, that of her children, and lifestyle. With disparate outlooks, there was no way that this relationship would come to a happy ending. Elle was disqualified from the start although she put a great deal of time into the relationship with Michael. Ultimately she could not make the compromises, as some women are able to do.

WOMEN WHO HAVE TO HAVE THEM

If a woman is fixated on landing this kind of man, she might think long and hard. Specific characteristics are as follows: He is obsessed with his success, driven to keep it up or to expand his enterprises. He has little time for his woman and inflexibility in terms of changing his methods. He always gets his way. The trade off is lifestyle and excitement, material possessions and travel.

There are women who have not remained with their money and power men and have come out on top. An example of a woman who pulled her life together after being married to a powerful man is Ivana Trump. When the news first broke, the tabloids painted Ivana as bereft that Donald had left her for Marla Maples. However, she soon reinvented herself, going on to publish novels, expand her business, and to remarry. Today she is every bit as public a figure as her ex-husband, perhaps more so.

As our society approaches the twenty-first century, physical power is no longer the yardstick to judge manliness. Men have had to create other avenues to exhibit their power. Muscles are no longer the end all and be all, and have been replaced with other values, that of sophistication, and intellectual pursuits. In the ever present search for more ways to reveal his money and power, the money and power man may end up in politics. The past few years have shown us Ross Perot, whose personal wealth made his campaign possible, and before that, the Kennedy clan.

Cars have become an extremely significant means to show the world a man's power and success. The love men exhibit for their cars begins at an early age and lasts a lifetime.

_____ Susan R. Shapiro and Michele Kasson, Ph.D.

> ## BOYS WITH TOYS
> *Be appropriately respectful of his toys*
> *Thank him profusely for any gift, and don't forget—he can afford it*
> *Be prepared to listen to his plans for his new possessions*
> *As his ornament, you must look the part*
> *His vision is narrow, the focus is on his possessions*

How many women remember their first boyfriend and his car? The dream of a car, symbolic of freedom and status, is lusted after. The money and power man may have a collection of impressive vehicles and care for them more than he does his partner, in enough cases. The car is also armor for this man, protecting him from the real world, another way of insuring him that he is special and elite. How he operates his car is another display of his ego and strength. Most money and power men like to race their cars —showing their fearlessness.

We could list the other boy toys which serve the same purpose: boats, planes, sports equipment, and women. Because men cannot wear much beyond a gold rolex watch and a pair of Tiffany cufflinks as a means to explain who they are, you may find yourself wearing the jewels, and shown to the world as his. Remember that the car, the clothing, the jewelry, and anything else that he possesses is not for you, but about him. If this attitude is acceptable, you are in luck.

Yvette met her money and power man during a summer on Lake Michigan. Having been single her entire adult life, at the age of forty-three she was ready for a committed relationship. Andrew, one of the boys with toys, was considered a prize bachelor. And Yvette was extremely flattered when he placed his attentions upon her. "In the beginning I felt very special being with him. He was so successful and loved to be with people. He traveled a lot for business and I went with him. I had no obligations and he liked that. I am a freelance researcher and my schedule is my own. We always went first class and stayed at the most elegant hotels. Andrew thrived on being with people and they seemed to adore him, they fell all over him. He had clients and staff at his feet. But it wasn't so easy when we were alone. It was as if he had a different hat on than when we were out in public. When we were at home he was difficult and stirred things up.

"If it was peaceful, he made a scene. He was irate and angry and needed ongoing adulation. I couldn't admire him constantly, without a break and that was what Andrew liked. He bought new things at a rapid rate — and became annoyed when I was unimpressed with his newest purchase, even if it was something for me. He was critical of my house and my car, but he wasn't willing to upgrade for me. I found his entire take on the material world to be twisted. Yet there was something about him, beyond the money and power that truly appealed to me, that kept me there. I had a feeling there had been plenty of others before me and if I left, there would be plenty of others afterward. That's why I stuck it out—my ego told me I could be the one."

Within a year's time, Yvette and Andrew were engaged. "I saw our engagement as ridiculous. By then we were fighting constantly and giving each other a hard time. Probably we had not shared the same view of the world and it had become a big problem. I became pregnant and had an abortion because I did not want his baby. That was when I knew that I could not love someone who behaved as he did. Yet I look back fondly on our time together, those trips and business dinners and I remind myself that it was an experience. There were times when Andrew was happy and could be very kind to me. That I miss. I think maybe it was partly my fault that I allowed the relationship to become an engagement because I was feeling incomplete without a partner. I put up with his attitude. His way of dealing with people all day spilled over to us. He was combative at work and also with me. I finally did not want the drama. Some women might because there is a high to it. I want to be shown that I'm loved, not abused and then showered with gifts when things are rough."

> **STRIKING A DEAL**
>
> *He's cheap with you but his ego demands he put on a show*
> *You anticipate his moods and behave accordingly*
> *You love him but you also love his power*
> *You stay, even though you find the existence hollow*

Often the woman who nurtures this partner does so because she is not powerful enough in her own right. She is sad and lonely whether she is with him or apart. She may be on edge and uneasy because she does not know where she stands. On the one hand she may be the recipient of a lifestyle which tells her that she is terrific, on the other hand, she may not feel this from her man, only from the showcase. She waits for this man's phone calls, subjugating herself and beginning to lose her essence. The money and power man cannot help but boss this partner around. He can deny that he behaves this way at the start of the relationship, but as time goes on he cannot help but exert his power over her.

As with any prey, the woman has been stalked out, lured. She has been hooked and lost in his world, to

> **THE M.O. OF THE MONEY AND POWER GUY**
>
> *He cannot detach from his work mode*
> *He thinks that women are fungible*
> *He claims to crave love and affection, but cannot give it back*
> *It is empty when he is alone with you*
> *You may feel pain but he is genuinely trying his best*

his method and expectation. In many cases, women lose the will for the relationship, because at the center it is hopeless and sorry. The money and power man has created a life that is all about him. For those money and power men who are divorced, one begins to wonder what the ex-wife would say and how she experienced their failed marriage.

The woman who is repeatedly drawn to the money and power man needs to set boundaries. If she is strong enough to stand up to this type of man, then his power can only benefit her. But if he undermines her work or belittles her, if he threatens her soul, crunching the very aspect he loved about her at the outset, she must think again. She must be honest with herself, and know that if she is there for money alone, it is a dangerous and empty place to be.

Jennifer has always been attracted to older men. Today, after divorcing her first money and power man because he couldn't be there, she finds herself entrenched in a second go round of the same nature. However, Dylan is a surgeon, and his power is combined with empathy and humanity. "I do not enjoy being single and this man is a wonderful companion. He makes enough money for the lifestyle that I want. I will be able to work at my job because I like it, without feeling the need to support myself. While being established in the work force has been a big part of my life, I can't keep up the pace, and I'm not certain a pressured job is feasible with the kind of man I like. I think he has to be the only important one. And that's fine with me.

"To be truthful, I'm tired of doing this, day in, day out. I am very attracted to this man's way of

> **WHAT MAKES HIM WHO HE IS**
> *Like most men, he yearns for acceptance and recognition*
> *He wants caring and love*
> *Everything centers around his self-esteem*
> *He must be the victor*

operating. I understand him and at thirty-eight, I'm more realistic in my expectations. I have already been with a man who bought me things instead of being there emotionally."

"Now I have found a potential partner who is just as powerful in the workplace but has real emotions. When he leaves for work it is not to make money for his clients, but to save lives. Of course, as a doctor who saves lives, he is often revered as a god. He is used to having his way, and even on weekends he wants it his way. I left my first marriage because the kind of man I was married to could not be there emotionally. I have found someone who can be. If a man has worked on his inner self, I want him. If he hasn't, I don't want him. There are so many unhappy men in the world, why bother, even if they have megabucks."

Dylan, with his unusual working hours, needed someone who could be attentive, and to provide a home life. The money and power man might not want a woman who seeks the spotlight. Whatever a particular money and power man desires in his mate, he usually gets. His work is at the center of his life and he is defined by it. His interests and lifestyle, whether he plays golf, pilots a plane, sails or skies, with homes to house the sport, are of great value to him. His wife, as his partner and his jewel, is expected to appreciate this pace and path.

WATCH OUT, YOU MIGHT GET WHAT YOU WISH FOR

The money and power guy drools over his latest conquest. If she stops admiring him for all of his toys, he will tire of her ways and find her as unhappy as the last.

In following the theme that a wife enhances your life, many power men want a female in their lives in order to be praised and envied by the outside world. She is a statement, a trophy wife, an object. He has his cars, homes, sports, toys, and his woman. How many times have we seen cartoons depicting the short, older, wealthy man riding in his red convertible with his tall, blonde girlfriend? Unfortunately, the cartoon makes fun of reality. For these men power equals money, and money equals the ornamental young female. The glamorous new girlfriend is his statement to the world of his worth. Too often this manifests in the break up of his marriage and the replacement with the latest version. These men continue to rush into new deals, bigger business propositions, as their prizes and rewards, financial and emotional, continue to propel them forward. Behind the curtain, these men are weak and longing for comfort. For some, they are unable to appreciate the support which is available, and instead seek out their fantasy.

Maddie, the mother of two little girls, was married to Herb for ten years. Herb was not a major player, but wanted to be. He made a decent living, while Maddie stayed home with the kids. She was very comfortable in her role as wife and mother, interested in politics, and finishing her master's program at a local university. "I saw my husband as a hard working businessman, who hoped that one day he would become a CEO. He needed to obtain the commensurate wealth, power, and status. When he started having an affair with a woman who worked in his office building, I was astonished. Both Herb and I have always been considered an attractive couple. She is several years younger than I, and very, very glamorous. When I asked him why he needed to do such a thing, he said that I was a good wife and mother, intelligent, competent, but that I just didn't have the right image. He told me that when he is with her, he feels like every other man envies him. I felt that he wouldn't have needed her if he was able to afford the Rolls Royce that he wanted. In the end this has cost him much more than the Rolls would have. He lost his wife and family in the pursuit of an ideal which I don't think has been realized."

While some men marry their new partners, and go on to raise a second family, just as frequently these liaisons end as the excitement of having a new, and often illicit relationship wears thin.

A BREED APART

The money and power man is not all bad. He requires understanding and patience. You must set your own limits, while allowing him to think it is all about him. If you can sustain this, you will win him over and keep him.

Charlotte has been concerned about the future of her relationship since her opportunity to marry a money and power man. At the age of forty-nine, and divorced, she felt she was well schooled in the world of men. When mutual friends fixed her up with Randy, she realized his type immediately. "He was dogmatic, powerful, serious and macho. The relationship became a love affair and I played it his way. For eight months it was glorious. Then he was to relocate for eighteen months to start another business. He doubted that I would wait for him. It was implied that I should come, but up to me to make the right noises. I found this odd. I think that he was so sure that anyone and everyone would follow his lead, that I was another one of the flock. But I wasn't thirty anymore and I wasn't going to do it so readily. He is very meticulous, a perfectionist. Fastidious actually. And a control freak. But his sense of loyalty to me went without question. And I knew that he wanted me there. He is in the public eye and his career is all encompassing. Today I am still deciding what to do.

"In some ways I am very guarded because he does not really validate my life. He comes first. There is a huge piece of who I am, with grown children and a grandchild, that means so much to me. He is exactly my age, without children. He doesn't really know my world and as interesting as he can be, I find myself keeping this from him instead of inviting him into my life. I know that ultimately it's my choice. I let him think it is his, but I know it is mine."

The glamour aspect of the money and power man works both ways. It keeps the woman there, putting up with his idiosyncrasies, and it also drives her away. The woman who regards her money and power man as limited and intangible has a better chance of success. For the woman who hopes for intimacy and a true partner, this man cannot come through.

DOES HE EXIST WITHOUT THE POWER?

He is not giving up his position of prestige and if he did, you'd be in terrific straits. He believes it is a war and he is in the trenches. Even his male friends are adversaries on some level. He will tell you frequently that he trusts no one. That is why he is where he is.

Stephanie lived for five years with a money and power man who was fifteen years her senior. Although they were business partners, it was not an equal partnership. "I lived with this man and worked beside him. It was a very tumultuous relationship. He took the position that we were equals but that some were more equal than others. When it came to personal relationships, he claimed that he knew more. He believed that he was superior in every way. He was grandiose. And I was only thirty-five at the time. Today, in my early fifties, I see how ludicrous it was for me to have taken his bunk. But he was also wonderful to me. And I would have married him, except that it wasn't a goal or interest of mine to be remarried. So much of marriage is a fantasy and I knew that this man was complicated. Eventually he treated me merely like a business partner and cheated me out of money I was owed. I saw how he had gotten to where he was. And I saw that as his partner, both in romance and in business, he was not fair or willing to give. I left him, although to this day I recall him as truly special and captivating."

Maintaining interpersonal power with a money and power man is an arduous and challenging task. But women are not powerless, even in the face of great power. They need only to realize their strength.

Dale felt that she needed to be on an equal footing with Frank. If he wasn't willing to accept this, then she wasn't going stick around. One can only maintain a relationship with an archetypal money and power man if she is not willing to relinquish her own value to bolster his. "We fell in love although I thought he was impossible. Everything had to be his way. I would stay at his apartment and travel home to my small children the next morning by limousine. After several months of this, I told him that I didn't think this was an appropriate arrangement. I wanted him to travel to me. He didn't love my terms, but accepted them. I was concerned about how much work it was for me to feel good, so I left the relationship and began to date someone else. He was not a money and power man and it was a relief. But Frank went crazy—he couldn't stand that I was able to resist him. He chased me down, he begged me to marry him. He told me to pick the house of my dreams and bring my children at once. I laughed at him. I knew it wasn't going to be successful unless we were going to take it slowly and work at it. Frank and I have been married now for two years, and it's been very happy. I know his limits and I know mine. There is nothing about his great success that turns my head. He knows that I don't need his money, or lifestyle, and that I'm in it for the feelings between us. This is the part of the marriage that we work on. It's always been so much easier for him to forget the feelings and just let his money buy the love."

Amelia's story is similar to Dale's in that both women were able to maintain their own feelings of power and importance when involved with their men. Amelia met Jared at a movie festival two summers ago and was drawn to him. Jared, a producer, was showing a film while Amelia was attending as a scout for a company. Once they were back in Los Angeles, they began to date. Within two months time it was an exclusive relationship.

"Jared and I are both in the film industry. It's the business where everyone has to be young and to be discovered. When I met Jared, he was fifty and frantic about his career. He had had several real successes and several flops, but certainly needed another success, his hour glass was running out. These Hollywood guys are so afraid of losing it all, that they need you to tell them how wonderful they are. I wasn't gaga about everything that Jared did. I wasn't in awe of him. I noticed that he would court writers and directors until the project was finished and then he'd drop them. Then I realized that it was how he treated women too. He couldn't pull off his power trip with me. He needed people stopping him on the street and in restaurants to say

YOUR POWER VS. HIS
Be prepared to walk away from the table
Remember that he cries out for inner rewards
Understand him better than he understands you
Let him know that you are the catch

Susan R. Shapiro and Michele Kasson, Ph.D.

> **IF YOU UNEXPECTEDLY FALL FOR HIM**
>
> *You must remember the genesis of his style*
>
> *What determines success is how desperately he has to have you*
>
> *Only you can decide how important you are in his life*
>
> *Only you can determine if this is where you want to be*

how great his last film was and I didn't pay much attention. I wanted substance from him. I think because I demanded it, it made a difference. At first he did not discuss my work, except when we were at dinner with people. So I let him know how good I feel about my work, and that it is every bit as important as his. Once we got the ground rules right, it made all of the difference. The money, cars and toys are in the background—something we both enjoy, but don't really take too seriously. In this business you're up or you're down. He would really miss all of the 'stuff' if we were down, but we've gotten ourselves prepared for that rainy day, which I hope never comes."

For all the money and power men who use their wealth and toys as a substitute for their self-esteem, there are those men who do not use it to drive their relationships with women. Their money is not used as a means of showing the world who they are. This man is an independent person regardless of his wallet.

In the case of Eliot and Louisa, Eliot's rise to great heights did not affect the relationship one iota. They are both in their mid-forties and living together for several years. Both come from lower middle-class backgrounds. Eliot had been through ups and downs in business, including a successful streak. Today he is involved in a venture which is about to reap the rewards he has been dreaming of. "Eliot and I share a view of the world. We are both secure in our values. Much of this comes from recognition of our roots. We've discussed the issue of money quite a bit, especially two years ago when neither of us were doing as well financially. Our attitude is good. We both see money as freedom to make choices, and nothing more."

7

*"True disputants are like true sportsmen,
their whole delight is in the pursuit."*
— Alexander Pope

CHAMPION SPORT/MACHO MAN

Forever ambitious and challenging, the champion sport/macho man has a remarkable desire to control his environment. This desire makes it nearly impossible for him to trust anyone else completely or to consider someone else to be totally competent. This especially applies to the women tossed across his arm. Be he a golfer or game shooter, the champion sport/macho man comes first and the woman comes second. We might find him in certain fields, the military, the police force, or an instructor for a sport. His dauntless approach to the world is very appealing to some women, others find this type to be belligerent and inconsiderate. What is outstanding about him is an almost Neanderthal quality that is enticing and has a raw edge— taking us back to a time before manners counted.

The play *Damn Yankees* opens to housewives lamenting the loss of their husbands to television during baseball season. One husband abandons his wife and sells his soul to

The Men Out There

> **PROTECTING HIS TURF**
> *He is loyal only to a chosen few*
> *His persona allows him to get his way*
> *He is difficult but can be sensitive—so we stick around*
> *Authority means little to him*
> *His own sense of entitlement keeps him focused*

the devil to regain his youth and obtain stardom by playing professional baseball. In the movies there are the acclaimed bad boys, Marlon Brando playing Stanley in *A Street Car Named Desire*, Clint Eastwood in *Dirty Harry*, Sean Connery as James Bond, is both bad and good, thus becoming daring, and Steve McQueen in *Bullet*. More recently, we pay to see Jean Claude Van Damme, Arnold Schwarzenegger, and Sly Stallone as macho heroes. We root for them even when we know what they are about. There is a crude, almost uncivilized allure that draws women to this type. But the antagonistic side of the champion sport/macho man may drive us to distraction. He struggles to sustain relationships with not only his partner, but with his co-workers, family members, and close friends. His behavior may be seen as self-defense, but how easily he is provoked is disheartening and creates tension and distance in the relationship.

EGO AND THE MACHO GUY

We know the stereotypes of the the Italian, Latin, or Israeli Lover. These men seduce the women, and at the same time they count on being worshipped. In exchange for protection and monetary comfort, the macho guy expects to be revered. His word is the final word.

Lucy, at the age of thirty-five, has spent the last four years involved with a champion sportsman. Although she and her partner have sought counseling, there has been little change in his attitude toward her. "I met Max when I was rock climbing. I should have known then. He was the bravest and most obsessed. And then he told me that he was a champion skier and loved to hang glide. I thought of him as acting out, willing to court danger. I love sports and to defy the odds myself. The attraction here is that we do great sports together. He and I have terrific energy and love a challenge. When we were first together, he told me that he'd met his match, that he wanted someone like me and that I was hard to find. The other women, he said, had been objects, who he came home to after a day of excitement. I am the trooper who will do it all with him. We have done some wild stuff, skied off limits, done black diamonds, and we want to go on a very challenging hiking trip next year.

"On the other hand, he is a selfish man who has to have to his way. He always tells me what to do and he can become angry over nothing. His temper is out of line. I dread his mood swings. I think he must have been abused as a child because he can be abusive and sniff out what he considers a threatening situation like he's some kind of police dog. So, when he's like that, I stay clear.

"I have told him how I feel about these moods. He knows that I won't stick around if he's going to belittle and demean me. He will praise me when I do something he thinks is fabulous and then put me down a few hours later. We race sports cars too, and it feels like he's competing with me. We can be on the open road and he's no longer my lover. Max becomes an enemy, and that is very frightening. He seems to forget who I am. I believe he would run me off the road. I really feel that Max tries to be good to me, but it's all about his territory and his being in charge of everything. I have worked hard to win his attention. I can't decide if he should have a traditional partner who yeses him to death or if I should fight long and hard for his affirmation."

The bravado recognized in macho men disguises their vulnerability and fears. They may overreact and become almost self destructive to prove they are not cowardly, but brave. The champion sport/macho man figure is one who has a keen sense of survival. Yet he imprisons himself in the world he creates, one in which he will not face his fears, but easily defends against them. His world is circumscribed and what he excels at is the sole focus. What other people say and their interests are of little appeal to him. Whatever form of his obsession, be it tennis, golf, watching football, building the biggest house, it's about putting up walls. Often this type of man will be obsessed with his membership at a country club or the health club as a way to avoid the empty parts of his life. His social life is comprised of sports and winning.

MACHO MEANS EGO MANIACAL

He seeks status to sate his ego. Superiority, in terms of sports, women or exclusivity, make him feel important. If he can excel, then he is ahead of the rest. In this case, his macho winning streak triumphs.

Jill met her champion sportsman at a party on the evening of her fiftieth birthday. He exuded a kind of charisma she couldn't resist and while women were "literally falling all over him", she was the winner. "I met Mark and there was this instant attraction. I knew that we would hit it off sexually but I was not attracted to his lifestyle. I could see it at once. He traveled in a pack and lived for sports. All that he and his friends spoke of that night were sports stories. I learned within an hour that he'd been a football star in college. This was a good twenty years ago, because he was about ten years younger than I. But he talked about it as if it had happened yesterday. I think his greatest regret was that he'd never made it to the big leagues. He was insecure and this apparently had shattered his ego. Then he made up for it by being obsessed with every sport you can name, from scuba diving to golf, to tennis, to skiing.

"He might have had a more artistic side, but he was afraid to show it. And he refused to reveal his sensitivity to me, even when we began to see each other regularly. He had a totally divided personality, where his feeling wild was connected to being macho and one of the guys. If he had a choice between me and the guys, he would always choose the guys. I have a suspicion that he'll never be married. Mark is jaded by the life he's carved out for himself. He has no respect for women. We were together for a year but I couldn't stand his priorities. No matter what the plan was, it was another sport to him. Where we'd meet, how we would be together, all of it was sport to him, a game."

Ultimately the relationship did not last because of Mark's lack of emotion. "I realized that there were no rewards. Winning him was losing him. I never allowed myself to truly care about Mark because I saw who he was. He was so jaded about sports and women that when we split he took up with women much younger than he—his latest conquest. I viewed him as a challenge and as great fun, but not for the long haul. My instincts told me that he was the type who would leave his wife at home and pretend that he is single. Who could deal with that? It's torture."

In our competitive society, the behavior of the macho man is endorsed. Women find his masculinity appealing in the hope that he is protector. We think of this partner as resilient and intrepid. Many times he will catch our eye in a public place, such as a bar or restaurant, or across the room at a party. At first he appears to be competitive, energetic, self reliant and tough minded. He perceives himself as strong and in charge. His superiority does not surface at once, and it is only with time that we can recognize this man.

Caroline met Lee at a Superbowl party where he sat in a chair and cheered, guzzling beer, for two hours straight. When he called the next day to ask her out, she was surprised he even remembered meeting her. "From the start there was this chemistry and I found him very upbeat. He had loads of energy and was not concerned with money. He did not seem bossy, as some men are. I think I must have been fooled, because in retrospect, he was extremely given to moods and would dominate any time it was possible.

"He loved to go hunting and fishing, to ski and to play baseball in this league from work. He lived for sports, to play or watch sports on TV. I also found him to be intelligent and he did well enough at his job as an office manager. His children, who were small boys, were pushed very hard by him to excel in sports. I felt sorry for them when we spoke about it, but he could not hear what I said. The way that he pressured his sons was the real indicator of who he was. I had a feeling that as they got older, it would get worse. He would be the kind of father who was the referee and would blow the whistle in his son's favor constantly. He was totally absorbed with how they did and his free time was devoted to his own sports.

> **DO YOU WORK FOR HIM?**
> *He will humiliate those who he employs, even the dry cleaner*
> *He has an unpleasant temper and is quick to be provoked*
> *He thinks he is superior to others, in all instances*

"I do not fish or ski and he did not intend to encourage me to try them out. As long as he excelled and I was there when he returned, it was enough. The one time I went fishing with him and his friends, he embarrassed me in front of everyone. I began to feel that Lee wanted me the way that I was, with his world being very separate from mine, and his macho sports taking up his Saturdays and Sundays. I wanted him to do things with me, but for a guy with his mentality, sharing with a partner doesn't even come close to being worth it. He hid behind his sports. Winning at a baseball game was more important than anything. I couldn't live like that."

What Caroline appreciated about Lee was his single mindedness. "I saw Lee's ability to concentrate on his sports and to win as a feat. I saw him as someone who had follow through. But that tough attitude wears you down, and I became tired of looking for emotional energy and finding none."

IDENTITY CRISIS

Men are no longer winning wars for survival or crossing the frontier, thus the way to exhibit manliness has been lost. Sports have become a way of showing that men are virile and accepted for their strength. Man's identity is tied into his champion sportsmanship. The desire to win and to belong is all encompassing. Since childhood these men have been influenced by sports and competition has been encouraged.

Boys begin playing sports as toddlers and remain entrenched in their sports until they die. For many boys/men a certain sport speaks to them, and the joy of being part of it is wonderful. It is when it is translated to everyday life that it becomes an issue. What makes a sport especially meaningful to a man is how he excels at it. He looks back and recalls how at the age of twenty he won a statewide tennis tournament which gave him credibility. He became someone to contend with, for the girls and for his home town. Having risen to stardom, the sense of validation remains long after his victory.

With age, a man's engagement in sports lessens and his

role as a spectator increases. The attachment to sports, however, does not die, but remains. Men see sports as symbolic of their lives. Yet in a sport, there is a winner or loser within a matter of hours and a referee to determine fair play. In a sense it is much more honest than in life, where there is much pretense and machismo played out in order to get through the day. *What is ironic is the fear of failure that pervades in sports and in life. That is a common denominator. Our society endorses the champion sports/macho man, and women accept this.* The football hero or basketball player is revered by both sexes, to a different extent. It is when a man excludes his partner for his love of sports that it becomes a problem.

Skye, at the age of thirty-eight, is married to a man who was a champion football player in college and has continued with the sport in their hometown in Arkansas. At the age of forty-one, he remains a champion sportsman to this day. "I cannot get Eric to give up his teams and his games for anything. While I don't want to interfere, they have absolutely taken over our lives. He is either out on the field with the kids, including our daughters, or he is in his own league with his buddies or he is lying down and clicking the remote control while his eyes glaze over. He watches sports events endlessly. There is little time left for me.

"I find he is grumpy when he's not at work or doing sports on some level. It's really strange. He is a big deal in our town because he wins every medal at the club. He is an excellent golfer and he also runs the basketball league. It gets in the way of our life together. On the other hand, at least he's in good shape and has some pleasure that is real. But he's so full of himself. I am definitely a golf widow on weekends. It sort of holds the marriage together and at the same time, makes me unhappy with him all of the time. I have decided that this year I will learn golf in order to be with him."

_____ Susan R. Shapiro and Michele Kasson, Ph.D.

For Ronnie, her interlude with the champion sports/macho man was a positive experience, despite her decision not to stay in the relationship. "At the age of forty-six I found myself divorced with three grown children. I began to date a man who was a few years older and seemed lovely but also very self-centered. He had been divorced for many years and I think that this situation creates a very selfish man. He was close to his two children but basically, he loved his freedom. I suspect that he never remarried because he really didn't want to share. But what he adored doing was playing sports, mostly golf and squash. He was extremely competitive and rigid with his time when it came to these sports. He would not bend his schedule to be with me, or to be with anyone. He had his games set up and he never changed the calendar. Since we live in Florida he was able to play golf all year round.

> **THE EFFECT OF SPORTS ON A MAN'S LIFE**
> He lives to win
> He makes time for them but not for you
> Only "real" men take it seriously
> When all else fails, sports are affirming

"Buddy and I got along very well as long as it was on his schedule. I was alone all Saturday and Sunday while he played golf. On Thursday nights he played squash and in the fall he was in a football league. He was too close minded to discuss this, but I was searching for a mate. I sat around while he played sports and saw life center around him, and what he wanted to do. If we had enjoyed the same things, it would have been successful. But he had an attitude. He did not really care about how I felt. During the week he worked hard in his business and on the weekends he played hard without me. If I spoke about these feelings, or any feelings for that matter, he would shut down.

"The reason that I finally decided I could not do this

was because of my ex-husband. I had been married to a very selfish man and I did not want to do it again. He was another type of man, but basically the message was the same. In the beginning it was very exciting, but after a few years, we stopped being together because it had grown lonely. He had let it slide. But I learned so much about myself from the relationship. I learned that I will never be with another man who does not validate me. It ebbs away at my self confidence. I have a need to be recognized. It might not be on the playing fields or at work, but it is a strong desire. I decided to take care of myself and that meant leaving Buddy. I explained to him that my needs were not being met. He did not respond. I admit, the sex was excellent, but I never felt any intimacy. It was sex for sport, it was another game that he was good at. I am grateful to the relationship for what it defined for me. I know that I require communication, empathy, sharing and that a man who is a sportsman and so filled with bravado could not do that. He only thought of himself and his winnings."

IF YOU WANT A FRIEND

The champion sport/macho man is not well schooled in the art of friendship. His defenses prohibit him from coming close to you and encourages a rigid outer shell. He would prefer to destroy a relationship than to change. If you have to have this particular man, understand his world.

Although work is a source of great self-esteem for men, and the role of the provider is intrinsic, there are those champion sport/macho men who feel that they are above the law. This is a method of covering up a sense of inadequacy, while showing muscle to the outside world. Their behavior is about decision and control. When his partner is more confident and self-assured than the man, it propels him toward aberrant behavior. The middle aged macho man may feel that he is losing it, even as he attempts to keep his life in order. He is shaken to the core. His arrogance is actually a facade for his insecurity, it is only through his sports and bravado that he can play for keeps. In the rest of his life, including the relationships that ought to be meaningful, he is posturing.

The final straw for Terry in her relationship with such a man occurred when she was in a car accident and her partner of three years, Adam, was unable to give her the support that she needed. "It finally hit home that he was not really there for me and could not empathize. Although I was not hurt, the car was totaled and I was very shaky. I left a message for him and he did come to my house. But he brought his friend, on their way to a soccer match. He said that he wanted to see if I was okay, but his 'seeing' lasted about ten minutes. That was it, I felt so abandoned and alone. I wanted him to put his arms around me and to stay awhile. I didn't need to hear his gruff voice and to watch his body language which showed how distant he was. It was a turning point for me. Things went downhill from then on. If I wasn't important enough during this upset, when would I be? I doubt that Adam saw it this way, or how much I needed him.

"He is a man's man and blind to a woman's feelings. He is very popular with the guys and has created a world for himself. Whatever he wants comes first, and people seem to jump because in his world, of soccer and lacrosse and all these leftover sports from college, he is the winner. So his cronies crowd around him. Adam was a great lover because he was accomplished, but when we were together in our life, out in public, there was something lacking. And he would lose his temper over small things. Yet he was the one who said that I sabotaged the relationship by not being

> **TELLTALE SIGNS OF THE CHAMPION SPORT/MACHO MAN**
> *He dehumanizes the relationship*
> *Sex is a sport like any other*
> *Beneath it all he is fragile*
> *His pride is at the center of his gamesmanship*
> *He fears the aging process*
> *His ego is tied up in the sports he plays*
> *He may love you but struggles to show affection*

interested in marriage. I doubted that he ever was, and I'd been in such a bad marriage, why would I want another? All I know is that whatever issues we might have had, once he did not act like a friend during the car crash incident, I didn't need him as a lover to show me his skills. It wasn't another game, it was about my life and I was very unnerved. We could only do it his way and ultimately, he didn't come through for me."

As a single man in mid-life, the champion sport/macho man searches for a partner while he is accustomed to running his own life. This life he has carved for himself is quite full and rich, focused on sports and the guys. Women are secondary and interesting only in small doses. If he has children, he will see them on schedule, but he is mostly preoccupied with his own life and work. It is usually his children's achievements that interest him. That aspect of their lives is something he most definitely can relate to.

The champion sport/macho man is alone and hunting for shelter without having a clue as to how to get there. He may fall short in many instances, but women are undeniably drawn to him. If a woman does not recognize her own strength, she will look to the macho man to provide the strength that she is missing or afraid to see in herself. What women admire most about the champion sport/macho man is his ability to plunge forward, without hesitation, into his sport, his work, his life. She usually fails to see the frightened boy inside. If she sees this and she still wants him, she has the opportunity for success.

TO HAVE YOUR REAL MAN

You must be prepared for his mood swings and constant incidents at work, during sports, at home with you. This is his nature. If you are willing to understand his fragile ego, a helplessness combined with a demand to be dominant and reckless, then you may proceed.

It is often believed that the ego plays a larger part in the life of men than for women in their lives. These men become counterphobic, challenging every sport and scenario that frightens them to prove to the world that they are indeed courageous and victorious. If they are heroic, they fail to recognize themselves as such, and continue to be immersed in self-doubt. The macho man needs to prove to the world that he has the skills and the ability to win.

Anita, at the age of forty-two, has been married three times. In her last marriage she encountered a champion sport/macho man. "I met John at a teacher's conference where we both were working. He definitely came on to me. I responded to his wanting me and to a continual wearing down of my defenses. He exhibited bravado and had to have it all his way. I assumed it was part of his culture. He was not good to me and still I stayed with him. I gave him my life knowing that he was a con artist. His sportsmanship was controlling me. I simply gave myself over because he thought I was such a thrilling game to play. As long as he was winning. This particular round consisted of my giving him all of my savings for our vacations and lifestyle. Whatever he needed he got, food, clothing, my car. And he no longer spent so much time on his martial arts. I think that the lifestyle that I provided was so comfortable that he decided to forego his past interests and pleasures. In return, there was endless sex and during the sex, promises of a great future. This was a future that never came to pass.

"I could see that I was in and out of denial with John. He was manipulative and temperamental. The sex kept me there. He was attentive and knew what to do. As I said, it was his latest sport. In his own sick way, he really did love me. It was an insane, romantic twist, it was not a relationship. Finally he got tired of our game and looked for a new sport. We split up after two years. But there had been so much that had been said that did not happen. I was devastated. He married the next woman, and in between he sharpened up his martial arts and became fit and seductive. Then he went on to the next prey. I suppose I was sort of cheated and also saved from a hellish existence.

"What I learned is that love is never enough. Now I know that seeing is believing. I don't believe in the dream but in the reality. Today I am stronger than ever before. Being with John while he performed his games on me was like being asleep. I was addicted to his games and he was addicted to them also. It was a charged and sick relationship that required a long recovery."

SOCIETY DICTATES TO THE CHAMPION SPORT/MACHO MAN

Since physical power is no longer the measure in the workplace, men seek it out for recreation. Yet their heroes continue to be the champion sportsmen themselves. These men are unable to move beyond the macho man as hero. No matter what emotion they feel, it is the sport, sex as sport, sport as sport, that appeals to them more.

Each champion in his field, Mohammed Ali as the boxing champion of the world, Magic Johnson as the basketball hero, or Mike Ditka as the football star, elicits a reverence from their male fans that is infinite. Men revere astronauts and mountain climbers. While muscle is no longer necessary to survive, men strive at sports, to win, to compete and to garner their power. The physical ideal is envied by all men, across the board, of all ages, religions and socioeconomic backgrounds. To be a champion sportsman is to be a warrior, and this above all, is respected. But physical power cannot alone make a man fearless.

Women often feel betrayed by this genre of man, because he believes in the passivity of women and the activity of men. He is the one who initiates in all areas of life, sports, women and work. Women are the receivers, cast in the traditional roles of care givers and nurturers. In the case of the champion sport/macho man, there is the expectation that she will be that and also be the achiever. This man appreciates winners, and considers himself to be one as well as the sports figures he roots for. The woman he decides upon will also be a winner. She becomes his trophy—another victory. A relationship may be seen as a war zone, with winners and losers. It is not likely that the champion sport/macho man will tolerate being the latter.

Alexandra's long standing live in arrangement with Zachary has been fraught from the start. They have put off an engagement three times because of Zachary's lifestyle and priorities. "I feel that I am involved with a man who is a boy for life. He watches football as if it is a life or death scenario. He pays no attention to me when there is any sport on TV or if his friends are around and they are talking sports or whatever they talk about. He is sexist and boyish. He both annoys me and amuses me. He can be very loving and gentle when we are alone together, but mostly he walks three paces ahead of me in public. He will

> **THE LONELY CHAMPION**
>
> He wants to be reinforced through his self-reliance
>
> He is not inhibited by danger
>
> Taking risks is exhilarating
>
> He is a loner, with a club of fellow macho men
>
> He is aggressive and arrogant
>
> He needs your love even when he is not connected

give up work days to go skiing or to go scuba diving, and will travel far away to get to those places. I do not have the clout to ask him to take a day off so that we can be together. I dread the rejection and so I do not even bring up the idea. But when we are alone together, we have a good time.

"When I first met Zachary, we spoke of getting married and having a family. I can only imagine what kind of father he would be to a son—especially if he didn't do sports as well as Zachary imagines he should. On the other hand, he might be a very good father, because he certainly is caring, in a gruff sort of way. He does many things that I do not like, such as smoking cigarettes, doing pot, chewing gum, wearing jeans constantly and looking like a lumber jack. I appreciate a casual look at times, but Zachary thinks he is the ad for Camel Cigarettes. He even smokes Camels. I complain about him now because I can't get through to him. He is impenetrable.

"I know that he loves me and he appreciates what I do. I run a nursery school that I've built up from scratch. I feel that I provide the stability in the relationship—I get up every morning and go to work. Some days Zachary will tell me that he's decided to take off to go rock climbing or kayaking. It's horrible. I look at him and wonder how he can do it. It's almost isolating, and off putting to anyone but his cronies who appreciate the same sort of stuff. At his job, he can plan his own schedule, but it seems so self-indulgent.

_____ Susan R. Shapiro and Michele Kasson, Ph.D.

On the other hand, he would be lost without these pleasures of his. And he loves the challenges. I don't know if we'll ever actually get married. I've given the relationship the best years of my life. I apply the 'devil you know' theory to us at this point. I suppose I do love him, and I accept him. What else can I do? Sports are his life and I can't compete. He only wants me when sports are not available, say on Thanksgiving day, in the morning, before the football games begin."

> **WHAT KEEPS YOU THERE**
> *He touches your heart*
> *You are comfortable with his priorities*
> *You have your own life that works*
> *You love some of his sports*
> *You recognize his vulnerability under the facade*

8

"Luck be a lady tonight..."
— GUYS AND DOLLS

THE WORKAHOLIC, SEXAHOLIC AND GAMBLING MAN

When a man is engaged in a compulsive behavior of one kind, it does not preclude him from having another addiction as well. For example, he may indulge in drugs and gambling, or sex addiction and drinking, or sex, drugs and rock and roll.

While the addict has been addressed in Chapter 5, his addiction is one which is chemically induced. In the case of the workaholic, sex addict or gambling man, his addiction is evoked by behavioral actions. The woman who chooses one of these types of men is often lonely and sad. She never truly has his attention, but a shadow of the possibility of an intimate relationship with him. The workaholic's tendencies are endorsed by our society and this addiction of the three, is the most honored. The workaholic smacks of the pejorative label of the alcoholic, but the paradox is that this man's behavior is often respected. The sex addict is a less obvious addiction, and while his male buddies might be privy to his frequencies, the women in his life are the last to learn. The gambler is a man who travels a roller coaster existence—his life may be enticing to his partner, but the blue Mondays are not easy.

The common thread for the woman immersed in a relationship with any of these men out there is their unavailability for intimacy. They are much too preoccupied to pay real attention to their lovers. What is curious is whether the addiction is a result of their inability to be intimate or whether the addiction precipitates the lack of intimacy. Recognizable in each category is a void within that cannot be filled by the lover, nor by the addiction. However, it is the addiction which these men seek for fulfillment and not the relationship with their women as a means for wholeness. The addiction is so central to their essence, that the denial of it is extraordinary.

THE WORKAHOLIC

The workaholic is often considered to be the classic Type A personality. These people are defined as driven and goal oriented, but lack patience and the capacity to suppress their feelings. There is a serious need for the workaholic man to control his world, which is one reason why he spends so many hours at work. He cannot relinquish any aspect of control to another, despite his employees with designated responsibilities. It is not uncommon for a workaholic to oversee the minute details when his time would be better spent elsewhere. If he does assign work to his employees, it is always with a supercritical eye.

Lynn's tale with her workaholic boyfriend of one year, Luke, has been very unsettling for her. At the beginning of the relationship, Lynn was unaware of Luke's compulsive need to work. In fact, he spent time with her in a manner that indicated that he was free and easy. Whenever they

Susan R. Shapiro and Michele Kasson, Ph.D.

had plans, he was attentive to her, it was only when she expected more time to be shared that it became apparent that he was totally entrenched in his business. By then, Lynn had fallen for Luke, and her emotions had the better of her. "What I wonder, as I look back on those early days, is if Luke did it on purpose. I mean, I know he loves me and wanted to be connected to someone but he really couldn't be without his business. He owns several stores that sell electronic equipment and he's become rather successful. I think he actually thrives on the idea of the stores being open seven days a week. If he could, he'd have them open twenty four hours a day. He struggled so when he first hired an office manager, he couldn't let go of the control. He has fired so many people in the short time that we've been together which is frightening to me. Always it was their fault. He is very critical because they could never work hard enough for him. No one fit his standards."

> **HOW TO SPOT THE WORKAHOLIC**
>
> *He really does stop at the office on Saturday night*
>
> *He is an early riser regardless of how little sleep he has had*
>
> *He writes notes to himself constantly*
>
> *He cannot tolerate idle time*
>
> *On vacation, play becomes work*
>
> *He keeps his cell phone on at the restaurant*

Lynn noticed that Luke's attitude extended to his children. "His first two sons were exactly like him. But the third child is a real renegade. He simply won't do what his father wants. What is strange is that Luke doesn't like that his sons work so hard. I can't figure that out. And when we first met, he told me that I worked too hard. I think that my view of my work, as a bookkeeper, is much more intact. In this relationship, it was Luke's way of working that got in the way. We were always on a schedule that was ruled by the stores. If it was a holiday weekend, he was crazy about his business and couldn't even see me. I felt that he was pushing me aside for his work. At one point I thought it was another woman, but it turned out to be this love of his work. It was much more rewarding for him than a love relationship because he is in charge. He would find fault with his employees and be in love with his business. I was always to the side."

WORK AS PROTECTION

There are certain workaholics who utilize work as a means to avoid anxiety. If their job is all consuming, they are protected from facing the real world. They spin a cocoon around themselves, which acts as a buffer for their feelings.

Lynn was the one who initiated the break up with Luke based on the fact that the situation did not improve. "I found with Luke that I made no impact. I would beg him to reconsider his time put into the company. I would ask him to spend a Saturday with me. Nothing worked and I found I had to give up the relationship, because I could not compete with his business. I felt so cheated with Luke, because I loved so much of what we had together. I loved his wit and his great energy. I just knew after the year that we could not become any closer. He had all these barriers, and the one that really stuck out was his obsession with the business. He also was quite preoccupied with his kids. But since I have no children, I'm not sure I was a judge of that. With the work situation, I knew it was bad news. I really want a life with someone, not just a slice of it."

Christine prides herself on being a hard worker, and this was a quality that she sought in her partner. After breaking an engagement at the age of twenty-five, she moved to Milwaukee, where she felt there would be more opportunity, both for work and love. Recently, as a thirty-nine

_____ Susan R. Shapiro and Michele Kasson, Ph.D.

year old single woman, Christine met Robert one night after work. "I was taken by his lifestyle, which he was able to afford as a commodities trader. Since I was on a career track as well, his values matched mine, and I thought that this

> **WHY THEY DO IT**
> *They have excess energy which needs a release*
> *Their success is their satisfaction*
> *There is an emptiness in their lives*
> *Adulation is guaranteed in work and may not be in other areas*
> *It is a way to avoid living life, whether conscious or not*

was going to be it. I didn't like Robert at first. I thought he was kind of nerdy, but he kept calling, and I guess he grew on me. I had great respect for him because of his job. It seemed that he fit in perfectly with what I wanted. He worked hard and was becoming more and more successful. I admired his incentive.

"He started to really make money, and lived in the kind of home that I always dreamed I would be in. I fantasized about how I would redecorate. On our dates we went to the places where we would be seen. But of course, there was one problem. Our dates were few and far between. He would call at midnight and ask if he could come over after work. He would wake me in the middle of the night, come over at four A.M., and then I would have to wake up at six to start my day. He slept till ten, and then worked all through the night again. He was always working, even when he was in a conversation with me. It took a while for me to figure it out. If I was on the phone with him, he seemed to answer everything correctly, but he was really not there. He was thinking about his work. He wasn't there with me, or for me. He had it down to a science, so that I wasn't quick to understand. I suspect that Robert did this with all of his women. He would listen to me but be figuring out a problem with his work. It took over his life. I only realized this after I had dated him awhile. He's extremely bright and he gets away with it with other people. By the time I left, I had become hooked on him while he remained hooked on his work."

NO ESCAPE

The workaholic prefers his work to anything in life. The personal satisfaction he derives from his work prohibits him from seeking much elsewhere. You, as his love object, suffer the consequences. There is little room for two loves in his life. His energy level is higher than in others, and he requires a means to release it. His work is the answer—it is his steady girl.

A famous workaholic is Henry Kissinger, former Secretary of State. He was known to concentrate on more than one important task at a time, and to spend innumerable hours on his projects. Another notable workaholic is Michael Milken, former head of Drexel Burnham, who at the height of his career was considered a genius who never slept. In the arts, we recognize prolific writers who, when interviewed, admit that they can write over fifteen hours a day. An excellent example of this is Stephen King. Jimmy Carter was admired for his ceaseless energy and endless hours put forth during his term as president.

THE IRONY

All of his life a man is encouraged to work hard and to make money. He is promised that his success will attract the right woman. In exchange, a woman is taught to work but often with the idea that she will marry and have a successful husband. When she lands one, lo and behold, he is all of that, but has no availability because in order to be a great success, he has boxed in his world. The more he desires love and attention

_____ Susan R. Shapiro and Michele Kasson, Ph.D.

from a woman, the harder he works to impress her. The harder he works, the more distant he becomes. She is left without a viable partner, while he has developed the habit of long hours at work.

Valerie, an executive secretary, has been with Chuck for the last three years. Today they are engaged to be married. "It's been a rocky road for several reasons. I'd say the most important reason is Chuck's schedule with his business. He has a mail order company that has taken off. What I find is that he works all Saturday and Sunday on this, and leaves little time for us, and none for recreation. One day I discovered that sex with me was planned in his date book, and I absolutely lost it. I was beside myself, but we laugh about it now. The key to making this relationship work is understanding who Chuck is, and that his addiction to work is simply a part of him that I can't deny. I have learned to make enormous efforts to put some time together."

If you are able to understand the motivation of the workaholic, and if you truly desire this man, it is wise to create a complete life for yourself which is separate from him. When married to the workaholic, women with young children become fully responsible for the domestic tasks and child rearing. As the children grow out of the nest, these women are at risk of suffering an overwhelming loneliness. They have not developed skills or a network of their own. Long ago their workaholic husbands disappeared, but this did not become noticeable for years afterward. It is a terrible loss for the workaholic husband and his wife that the precedent has been set. *Such tales can be avoided if both partners understand the nature of the relationship with a workaholic.*

In the case of Margo and Troy, Troy's workaholism was overcome when Margo threatened to leave the relationship. "By the time I had turned forty, I was no longer happy to be

> **WORK AND PLAY**
> Do not ask for the unattainable
> Schedule trips that entice him
> Do not keep him away from his work for too long
> Create your own life
> Do not attempt to delegate domestic responsibilities
> Tie him to you by giving him the rope

with someone who put in the kind of hours that Troy did. He is a dentist who is devoted to his patients. They come first without question. But what really bothered me over the years was his dedication to the practice. He is a good guy, but he is not exactly exciting and I have decided that it has to do with his work. Dentists are not wild or crazy, yet Troy is a wonderful man. If I did not bug him, he'd never come home and would do his paperwork through the night. If a patient calls and has a crisis at three in the morning, Troy opens up the office. He has become very successful as a result but he's so rigid. It takes away any passion from our relationship. I have told him recently that I will leave if he cannot give us some energy. He has finally heard me and I believe we are in better shape for it. Not that he's going to alter his schedule completely but he is definitely going to try. That means a lot to me. I have decided to stick it out and to attempt to be less frustrated by his hours."

THE SEX ADDICT

The sex addict is another kettle of fish from the workaholic, but the concept of addiction remains. The underlying motivation for the sex addict is similar to that of the workaholic/gambler in that this person is seeking to fill an empty place in his life. Rather than using work as the medium, this man seeks out physical relationships with women. The relationships become a compulsion. What separates them from other men in physical relationships with women is the need

_____ Susan R. Shapiro and Michele Kasson, Ph.D.

for conquest, variety, and endless mastery. The sex addict is not as visible as his cohorts in addiction and for the women who line up with this kind, it is a private hell at times. The sex addict has a vacant center which he chooses to fill with his triumphs. The lack of significance in any of his relationships continues his cycle, the search for a woman who can ameliorate his loneliness. This woman suffers the consequences of her partners' search—he cannot connect except through sex. While the sex seems prolific and unending, there are problems. At the extreme end of the continuum is the sex addict who must constantly obtain physical relief.

When it comes to sex, the double standard still exists. Little boys are taught the ideal of obtaining women. The sex addicted man is not someone who has on occasion cheated on his partner nor does he have one night stands. Rather, this man is someone who does so repeatedly and cannot stop. His behavior is compulsive, and often destructive to those around him. However, women do want this man because he is exciting, a challenge, sexually charged, and she harbors the hope that she can be the one to lure him. Or she may be in it just for the moment herself and his pattern is acceptable to her. In this situation, it works for both the man and the woman.

When Monica, an emergency room nurse, met Jude, she was thirty-nine years old and divorced without any children. Jude, the managing director of an ad agency, quickly explained to Monica that women attached themselves to him and that he did not return the favor. "He made it clear from the start that any

THE EXTREMIST

He is totally obsessed with his sexuality
He talks to everyone about sex
He is never without his porno
When not with a woman, he must masturbate
He lusts after anything in a skirt

expectation on my part would be an error. He set the rules and I respected them. Mostly we would go to dinner or to the movies. For hours and hours afterward we would have sex. At first I was really flattered by the kind of sex it was—almost bottomless sex. It was as if he'd been schooled somewhere other than in this country. He knew an amazing amount and was so attentive to me. Then he became crazy. He had these fetishes. I had to do certain things in certain ways. If I varied at all, he went berserk. It was really frightening. There was never a time that I saw Jude that we didn't have sex. He told me he was addicted to our sex. I suspect he was addicted to sex and I was his latest number. This lasted for two months and then I think he tired of me. I know that I learned something from our tryst. I am now very wary of a man who only wants sex, no matter how giving he seems to be, or how accomplished he seems. It isn't where I want to be."

The underlying motivation for the sex addict is that he has a need for sexual stimulation. Our society acknowledges a male's need to fulfill his sexual appetite, while women are not usually expected to have such a need. The initial sense of a highly charged sexual tryst may be thrilling, but once you become his, you realize what it is about. Neither of you may be able to sustain the relationship for too long.

In Betty's situation with Donald, his sexual addiction has not abated over the thirteen years that they have been married. Both are thirty-eight years old and the parents of two children. "From the beginning of my marriage, there has been an amazing amount of sex. Donald has always wanted and expected it. When the children were small and I was very tired at night, he did not seem to care. I remember those nights right after the babies were born, when I was ragged and Donald wanted hours of sexual fulfillment. I begged him to go easy but he told me he has this insatiable sex drive and wanted me at any hour of the the day. I found it tiresome and almost odd. In my efforts to keep the marriage alive, I have promised not to turn him down, no matter how I feel. The part of the deal he has to keep is that he won't go to other women. He fantasizes about other women instead. And he has *Playboy* and girl magazines and goes to strip joints where there are topless and bottomless women. If you ask me how I feel about it, I admit, I've pushed it aside. He is a good husband and a good father and I love him. But it's not easy dealing with all the sex and all the expectation. In a way I'm also addicted to his addiction. It is still a bit much, but I feel appreciated and I see Donald as an exciting man because of his sex drive. I know without the sex there wouldn't be any marriage at all."

WHY WOMEN WANT HIM

He is enticing and glamorous. His seduction is without end. You want the goods he is selling. He holds the curtain and there is a kind of perpetual attraction. And he's a pro, he has really honed his skills. If a woman is ripe for the challenge, it is a feather in her feminine cap.

THE GAMBLER

The gambler conjures up an image of a dangerous risk taker who is also suave and sophisticated. The most revered gambler of all is James Bond, 007, as he collects his chips, and the beautiful women in exotic locations. The reality of the life of the gambler is quite unlike that of 007. Yet this man, like James Bond, lives on the edge and thrives on the excitement. His life is comprised of winning and losing, and waiting for the next win. He reclaims the victory in order to take the gamble again. If he loses money he must make it back, if he wins, the stakes are raised. The woman in his life is always put to the side despite that the lifestyle is seductive. She's present for the highs, the material goods that result after a win, and his public persona which is quite alluring.

A woman is shown a good time by the gambler depending upon his mood and finances. As his winning escalates, she becomes the recipient of his good luck. She receives a shower of material items, and fancy dinners, and is able to share in the spillover of his excitement and zest for life. At first she may not realize how involved in gambling her partner is. When dating, he keeps his gambling life apart from her, except for those times when he wishes her to accompany him. She has no reason to suspect there is a problem at the outset because she is not involved with him on a daily basis. The situation is different for the woman whose man becomes a compulsive gambler after they are in an established relationship.

In the realm of the gambling man, his style is determined by his ability to think magically. In other words, what he wishes to happen, must happen. When he wishes to win, and does, his world is in order. When he loses, there is disbelief followed by the compulsion to gamble again and this time, to win. In the same way that he doesn't realize how he reacts to his gambling, he does not recognize how he treats the woman in his life. Whether she is his lover, spouse or new found friend, there is little room

> **THE WARNING SIGNS**
> *His ego is frail, he cannot tolerate disapproval*
> *He is impulsive and has to have immediate gratification*
> *He may be overanxious*
> *He wants to win-and expects it to happen*
> *He craves excitement and stimulation*

Susan R. Shapiro and Michele Kasson, Ph.D.

for a significant relationship. He is consumed with his addiction.

Rebecca and her husband, Tyler, were married for twenty-five years before she discovered that he was a gambler. At the age of fifty, Rebecca is now alone and divorced from Tyler due to his gambling addiction. "Tyler was the quietest, most wonderful of husbands, he was loving, sociable and even tempered. We had a terrific relationship and I had no idea that he had a love greater than his love for me. I never saw his pay check and I never balanced the check book. Money was his domain. Every once in a while he would surprise me with jewelry, a fur coat, season tickets to sporting events, or some other totally unnecessary treat that let me know that life was good to us. Then one night my whole life changed when Tyler never came home. I was so worried that I called the police and the hospitals. But there was no accident. He had run off, leaving me to pay his debts. We are not together anymore, and I still find it hard to believe that this could have happened.

"When I look back I realize that there were signs all along, but I closed my eyes to them. Before he left, he had periods of being hostile and on edge all of the time. This was so out of character for my gentle mannered husband. It must have occurred because he was on a losing streak. He also started keeping to himself, asking me to go on

> **TELL TALE SIGNS**
>
> *He is borrowing money from you or others*
>
> *He displays a temper that you've never or rarely seen*
>
> *He has become anxious*
>
> *He frequents sports events, when he has rarely done so in the past*
>
> *He doesn't look friendly when the neighbors place friendly bets*
>
> *His routine has recently changed*
>
> *He's secretive about money*
>
> *He is suddenly avoiding certain friends*

errands for him, I believe to have some privacy. Then the phone didn't stop ringing. People that I had never met, and names I never heard, were asking for Tyler. And we also stopped going out to do things. He remained at home, by the TV, often watching sports. I can only guess that it was to find the results of games that he had bet on. Looking back, the pieces fall into place, but when it was happening I didn't understand it, it was so foreign to me. I did not want to accept that something terrible was happening in my marriage."

The gambler is not likely to quit his addiction on his own. If you become attached to a man and you realize he is a heavy gambler, it is wise to rethink the attachment and to envision your future realistically. He will never be there for you unless he is able to seek help and to give up the habit. You will witness him borrowing money from you and from his friends. Even when you confront him, there will be denial. While Hollywood has portrayed the gambler as a romantic hero, in such illustrious films as *The Hustler* and *The Color of Money* we need to remember that real life is not the movies. Your gambling man can easily break your heart.

> **WHAT YOU CAN AND CANNOT HAVE**
> *Your life will not be consistent*
> *He will be unreliable*
> *It will not be a wholesome existence*
> *He will encourage you to aid in his addiction*
> *He will love you outside the arena of his addiction*
> *He may go into treatment for your sake*

Although Kay found time with her gambling man to be thrilling, and saw Dennis as a terrific mate, she also knew from the first day that he was an addicted gambler. "When he drank, it became worse. He was a big gambler and a big drinker and the nights in the casinos were unbelievable

_____ Susan R. Shapiro and Michele Kasson, Ph.D.

highs but the morning after was hell on earth. I loved him desperately but I couldn't change him. He wouldn't even listen to me. And after three years of this, I left. I want a stable life and Dennis couldn't even think about it. I never knew which was worse, the drinking or the gambling. But there is something about the combination that is so deadly. Today I hear that he was in rehab and has married and has a baby. So, I suppose he was educable and another woman had the opportunity. But I wasn't able to change him one iota."

The workaholic, the sex addict, and the gambling man all suffer from addictions which are disorders of impulse control. With each man, there is the impulse which he cannot contain because of an underlying need, his lack of self-esteem and his hurt ego. He does not feel worthy and so these addictions become his vice. He is frightened to be an adult and his impatient nature and need for pleasure drive him to whatever his addiction may be. We must remember when we are with these men that they desire affection and approval, they require recognition.

YOUR ROLE IN THE DRAMA

While he may struggle to obtain it through fantasy and illusion, you are not part of his escape but a side bar to his life. Not every tale ends badly, but one must enter the world of the addicted man with complete knowledge of what the obstacles are.

Part III

Sex and Love

9

"From forty till fifty a man is at heart either a stoic or a satyr."
— Sir Arthur Wing Pinero

THE STOIC/WOMAN AS OBJET d'ART

The stoic is a man who has resisted his feelings for a very long time. As a result it is difficult to penetrate beneath the surface. Women find him to be distant and remote while he is also solid, caring and has great sex appeal. He yearns to be connected and to this end he will do the right thing. But his life is comprised of gestures, he is not truly feeling but going through the motions. He is an automaton, unable to be romantic or feeling because his desire is only on the surface. If your partner is a stoic, you will find that he intellectualizes all that goes on in his life. While he seems able to handle everything, it is only because he is not attached that he succeeds. This characterisitic extends to his view of women. He very much wants a woman in his life, and yet the physical relationship mirrors the lack of emotional relationship. *It is depersonalized, emotionless, routine and* unattached. *This is not intentional but stems from his lack of emotional depth and intimacy.*

In ancient Greece, the Stoics had four virtues to be recognized, that of practical wisdom, justice, courage and self-control. They were expected to use their intelligence to keep their emotions at bay. Using their intelligence served these men well, to be fair and even tempered and to have the ability to consider a situation carefully before reacting. A futuristic stoic is that of Mr. Spock from *Star Trek*, a man who saves the day and is depended upon to find the proper solution. However, he is emotionless and does not react from the heart. *The man out there who is a stoic can handle it all, whatever life throws out to him.* While there is no need to demonstrate physical strength in today's world, where we are urbanized, there is still the expected male competence. In the civilized work place, he must handle the emergencies and crises on a daily basis. The ideal is the even tempered and unflappable man. His stoicism is exhibited by his cool exterior in the face of great turmoil.

The woman beside this man is enamored of him. She fails to see, initially, that he is robotic and unable to really care. He has trained himself to be coolly dispassionate in order to achieve a mastery over his environment. The stoic is a modern day hero because our society endorses his act. He promotes the skills that are sought in the market place. What we must remember is that his priority is not you, despite his longing for an attachment. As in the case of Mr. Spock, this man lacks the hard wiring necessary to attach to a partner. The sex, as a great measure of one's feelings, is thus empty and digital. His efforts are there and often he is solicitous. The stoic/objet d'art man is a tough one to spot immediately.

When Iris met Russ, she was intrigued with his demeanor. Having weathered a severe emotional storm in

_____ Susan R. Shapiro and Michele Kasson, Ph.D.

a divorce, she admired a man who appeared to be a rock. His own divorce did not flap him and his ability to be centered was striking to Iris. "I had never met anyone like Russ in my life. He seemed to be so sure of things and nothing ever really upset him. If there was a problem, he figured out a solution and made it look so easy. Compared to my own histrionics over my divorce, I was taken in at once. We spent many months together but I really never got to know him. He remained the same, being a person who never sensed a crisis, and instead took care of everything. His own marriage had failed because he was unattached emotionally. In our relationship he worked hard at becoming the romantic. It took me a long time to figure out why I wasn't happy because he did everything right. I kept wondering why it didn't work for me. Then I realized that I was responding to how hard he was working at the romance rather than feeling the romance itself.

> ### THE ROBOT IN HIM
> *He seems to listen, but he's really calculating a solution to something else*
> *He does what is expected, but that's exactly what it feels like*
> *He is pleasant, but passionless*
> *Sex is technically correct, but lacks lust*
> *His environment is sterile*

"The issues with Russ extended to our sex life. He did it all, but not because he had all the moves to please me. It was more like he had read a sex manual. First he did this, then he did that. But the longing wasn't there. I sensed this from the beginning. At first I thought he was perhaps a little naive, then I realized that he was unimaginative. I struggled with how to leave this sensational man who did everything right. He was good looking, and had a good job. He wanted me, he was strong and tough minded. He solved all my problems, so why didn't I want him? The answer was, because he didn't make me feel anything."

The Men Out There

The stoic in Western Culture is the boy who cannot remain in the boy's body. He becomes a man in a society that does not define him. He is the strong silent type who has no war to win and thus his place in his career and his sexuality become the measure. The women in his life are objects, not purposely, but due to his own limitations. And in some cases his children are objects also, because this is his only way to relate. He is the civilized hero, who abides everything. However, his absence is at the core of problem, and it is the external world that functions for him, not his personal relationships.

On the silver screen we have stoics, as well as macho men. In *True Lies*, Arnold Schwarzenegger plays the role of a man, who in the service of his career, must sever his emotional ties to his family. But we see at the end that he is able to rekindle his feelings. In the movie *Seven*, Brad Pitt plays the part of a detective who is virtually unattached from the crime he is investigating. It is only at the very end when his wife is murdered and her head handed to him in a box, that he emotes, coming to life. Few of us in the real world become involved with a spy or a homicide detective. It is the every day man who is stoic in nature that baffles his partner. As in Iris's story, stoicism is not readily deciphered in a man who has it all under control.

NOT EASY TO SPOT

The stoic/objet d'art can be rigid even while he's accommodating. His responses are mechanical, and he may view displays of emotion as silly and immature. At the same time, he is a good listener, who is empathic at arms length. He definitely wants you, but you are also kept at a distance.

Laura, at the age of thirty-five is a teacher in Hartford, Connecticut. Divorced for three years, she has been in an

Susan R. Shapiro and Michele Kasson, Ph.D.

unhappy relationship with a stoic/objet d'art man for the past two years. "Rick is several years older than I and has two children. I have one child who he chooses to ignore. Frankly, I think he ignores his own children too. He takes care of them financially, and makes sure they have all of the items they need, but they don't have a father. I find him self-centered, but I can't put my finger on it. I don't love him, and there's no future we can plan together, but he has an appeal. The sex is great because he's very accomplished, but he's not there emotionally. He doesn't want the responsibility for my emotions or for his. The sexual intimacy has not grown. Although we do things together like play tennis or cook, the rule is that we are not allowed to listen to each other's pain. He has no empathy, no compassion, no regard for my life, yet to the outside world, he's a great guy.

> **PORTRAIT OF A STOIC/OBJET D'ART**
> He's not introspective
> He's steadfast
> Fun is not important to him
> He refrains from social contact
> He has peripheral relationships
> He is expressionless

"The worst part is that he's a nerd. It is almost like he has missed a beat and he can't catch up. He has a group of friends, but he seems to always be on the periphery. I bet that when he was in high school he must have been one of those who walked around with a plastic liner in his shirt pocket. He's the type that would have been collecting butterflies rather than playing on the football team. Yet, as a man he has developed this strength. I am pulled into it again and again."

As in any category in *The Men Out There* a range of behaviors is available to the stoic. In a mild form, you may note the stoic/objet d'art participating in a group but never being at the center. In a more extreme case, he may forgo his friendships, to concentrate primarily on a solitary activity. Even the stoic's hobbies are isolating. For instance, he will collect coins or take bike rides, but will not participate in a group activity. He approaches life much in this fashion— alone and with a stiff upper lip. For his partner, there is a long period of adjustment to this kind of behavior. If her personality style is one where she too refrains from involvements, their relationship can only be hollow. If she is a very social and vibrant person, then she brings to the table what he cannot provide. While she may be frustrated with him, she may also be content to fill in the missing pieces.

The situation between Fran and Mitch was fraught from the get go. Fran, divorced with two children, was introduced to Mitchell at a business dinner. Mitchell called the next day to ask her out, and they dated exclusively for three months. "Mitch told me in the beginning that he had dated many women since his divorce three years ago. I should have listened carefully because the common thread was that every time he and his partner had the possibility of getting closer, he became disinterested. Mitch was after someone who had accomplishments, independence, and didn't scratch the surface of who he really was. He listened to my story and was politically correct, but it felt like he had been taught, like it was rote. I had this feeling that there was an invisible fence between us that he kept up.

"He was very deliberate in how he went about the relationship. Every action was appropriate. He was gentlemanly, and considerate, but he wasn't emotionally engaged. Nothing seemed to bother him, or if he became aggravated, he still had this smile painted on his face, as if to say everything is under control. I thought he cared about me, but I don't think he can genuinely care about anyone. I feel like he was a soldier who had built a fortress. I was invited to visit, but never to stay. There wasn't even a glimpse of who he was, just all of this armor.

> **THE SELF-PERCEPTION**
> *He yearns to connect*
> *He does not understand how crippled he is*
> *He sees himself as industrious and serious*
> *He will defend against intimacy*
> *He believes that he handles any curve ball*

"The sex was a big part of the relationship. I found it almost frightening. He took condoms out of the drawer like he had done it too many times. He knew how to do it all, but it was without feelings. He could have cared less about me, yet he wanted me. The sex had no love. He did not hold me afterward. It was politically correct sex. He touched me in the right places, at the right time, in the right way. I really cared for him and I needed him to respond, but he couldn't. When we were out in public, he would hold my hand, yet he didn't mean that either. It was one of the strangest relationships I've ever had. In the end, we agreed that we couldn't take it anywhere else and decided to part."

The stoic/objet d'art views emotion as a way to lose himself. He withdraws and does not have to face his feelings. Masculine tenets in our society condition men to believe that women come second and never first. Work is more significant than a relationship, as are the hours put forth with male friends. In the life of the stoic, there is no real connection anywhere but the priorities remain the same. The respectful demeanor and habits of the stoic often mislead his partner. He holds it altogether but he has such high walls, it is difficult, if not impossible, to penetrate.

In a relationship, you may perceive a problem, but he is bewildered at the mention of one. He says that he loves you, and he feels that he does, but you don't feel it. Your experience is miles apart from his. You do not feel that there is an equal partnership in intimacy. While he does activities with you, you don't feel the sharing of joy, of excitement, or even of disappointment. Therefore, you feel a lack of connection.

Erica was quite smitten with her stoic/objet d'art man, Seymour. Yet the relationship was unnerving and frustrating. Regardless of what Erica did or did not do, she felt that she could not get Seymour's attention. "I can no longer be with someone who simply won't acknowledge me. It isn't that he treats me unfairly but he simply doesn't consider me, or factor me into the equation. It's as if I don't count. When we go out together, he is always very proud of me and I know that he wants someone with credentials. I am a banker and have some interesting clients. Seymour has a lifestyle that is enhanced by my work. This matters, but mostly what matters is that he does everything correctly and it all looks right, feels right to him, even. But not to me. He is considered a great guy, except that no one really knows him. It is impossible to understand how Seymour ticks, because he is so guarded. Everything about the time we spend together is perfect and empty at once. I think about leaving him half of the time. Then I remember how much he needs me and that it almost isn't his fault, it's just the best that he can do."

> **WARNING SIGNS**
> *If you feel like you love him more than he loves you*
> *If you tell him how you feel more than he tells you*
> *If you say I love you first, on a constant basis*
> *If he backs off when you want to discuss the relationship*
> *If there is sex without any intimacy*
> *If there is no physical contact except for the sake of sex*

Seymour is very strict with Erica in terms of money. "He has taken care of the finances since early on in the relationship. He watches over everything. It isn't only about control, I suspect, but about the way that he has chosen to live. He believes that if one is always polite and correct, in any circumstance, they are a success. He can't possibly feel, he can only react. It's difficult at times but I know that he loves me in his own way. Perhaps if we have children, he'll come more to life. I know that he is proud of me—this is important to him. So I'm sure he will be proud of our children. I only hope that he can be flexible with them."

It may be that the stoic/objet d'art is not truly without feeling but without the ability to express these feelings. He is crippled when it comes to talking about his emotions and the only way to get him to react is to have a practice session. In other words, if your stoic was granted the opportunity to act out his feelings, as if on stage with a script in hand, he might acquire the skills to do it in real life. As he now proceeds in life, this man is unable to differentiate between his emotions. When he does emote, he is astonished and troubled. His social life is limited and not at the forefront of his existence. He does not see the subtleties of life.

Caroline actually found her stoic/objet d'art man to be boring. Together for over two years, Pierre, at the age of thirty-eight, is divorced without children, and an officer in the military. Caroline, an occupational therapist, at the age of thirty-five has never been married. Today they are engaged. "When I first met Pierre, I thought of him as some kind of savior. I was very sad, having just lost my mother. He was extremely supportive and strong. He never once flinched when I was falling apart. On a bad day I was hysterical and out of line, but Pierre was a rock. He encouraged me to go back to work and to not stay at home and mourn after the first week. I was able to do it, and because of him, I believed that I would get through. This was when we began dating, and I really knew very little about him.

The Men Out There

"We dated very cautiously at first. He set the pace and had a particular way of doing things. Even in conversation, he expected me to wait until he had finished his complete thought before I could respond. When we were alone together, in the beginning, this was fine. But when we were with people, it was uncomfortable. He is very well regarded on the base and has an excellent reputation. Definitely Pierre is someone who commands respect. However, our life together is very circumscribed. Never has Pierre shown me how he really feels. And when we're in bed together, I think I could be any woman, that it isn't about me in particular. This is very upsetting to me. I think I could disappear and that he would only notice because a woman is supposed to lie beneath him. Any woman."

HOW HE SUFFICES

He often works at something mechanical or electronic, and has little contact with others. He will show minimal responsiveness to events which will provoke emotions in others. He may seem to lack vitality or spontaneity. Anything that he does that is spur of the moment seems like an enormous achievement to him. He is aloof or remote when he is required to react. He may appear naive and superficial. He will not exhibit anger or joy.

He has a strong ego but there is no closeness with the stoic/objet d'art man. Becoming angry at this man won't work, and you will simply be pushing him away. He will not be chastised for his ways. Attempting to persuade him won't succeed either. He will realize that you are trying to influence him. You cannot attempt to show this man what is wrong. He does not take responsibility for his behavior. If you cannot survive without him, and refuse to avoid him, be prepared. He will not alter his ways easily or readily.

_____ Susan R. Shapiro and Michele Kasson, Ph.D.

Natasha and Wally, both at the age of forty-one, have recently had a child together. Although Wally felt the need to marry in order to have a baby, Natasha refused. "I explained to Wally that I do not want to be married to him. I knew as soon as I discovered that I was pregnant, unexpectedly, that this was a tremendous opportunity and that at my age it might not happen again. Wally agreed to support my decision, but he was perturbed. He really believes in the right thing and has this sort of heroic way of going through life. To not marry me means he will not be my hero. And he also cannot show me off to his clients in quite the same way because I have done something that is considered less than ideal. On the other hand, his weird code which he lives by is what keeps him beside me. He is a hero in his own eyes if he did not abandon me because I was pregnant. A part of his code is that you never flinch in the face of a disaster but you make a decision and stick by it. That is exactly what he has done in our situation.

"Yet he is so difficult at times that I really cannot marry him. He is wonderful in public and great at his job but he's so bottled up. I can never get him to talk about anything that matters. Or doesn't matter. He's mostly silent. He doesn't see his way as wrong, but I tell I him how shut out I feel. He is not superficial, but unwilling to let me in. Or anyone else. There are no highs or lows in our relationship, we sort of go along. Now with the baby, he wants to be married. He says it doesn't matter ultimately, but again, he's just showing his stiff upper lip. He will eventually go crazy because we are not married. I

HOW TO WIN OVER YOUR STOIC/OBJET D'ART MAN

Know that he has little insight into you and your priorities

Accept that he will not take responsibility for his emotional behavior

Be ready for a lack of response

know it. It's not about image but about the right thing. And it isn't about loving me enough, because he can't love me enough. It isn't his fault, this is who he is. That is why I am waiting to see if it is what I want."

The stoic is not a man who reacts with fear, and may not be cautious in a potentially dangerous situation. This distancing from fear extends to other emotions. For the woman he is involved with, there is a sense that his ability to be affectionate is dulled and stymied. While a woman will most likely be irritated with this type of man, he is not unhappy with himself. His satisfaction with his life as aloof or distant is acceptable to him. It is the love object who is continually let down and hopeful that more is ahead. If you, as his partner, believe that if you dig deep enough you will get the desired result, you are being naive. This man intellectualizes his ways, and is able to explain his mode in very confident terms. Any emotional issue is approached from an impersonal, and mechanical perspective. If the woman he chooses is able to accept this, and to contribute enough emotional energy and reaction for two, there is a shot that things will move forward. If she marries this man, he will concentrate on the formal and objective pieces of the wedding; the cost of the party, the deadline for the invitation, and not the happiness of embarking on the second half of his life with the partner of his choice. It seems that he cannot focus on the personal, inner meaning of events or relationships.

For Beth, Calvin's attitude was acceptable, because she recognized his needs from the start of their relationship. "At the age of forty-three, I met a man who was twenty years older than I. He was very set in his ways and had a certain lifestyle and a certain rule for everything. It was a healthy relationship sex wise, but I felt as if he'd done what we did together a thousand times before. He was

_____ Susan R. Shapiro and Michele Kasson, Ph.D.

very experienced at giving me pleasure even though there was a missing center piece. With Calvin, I knew that the sex was important because he'd been taught that it was. I was not in love with him, but I was in lust with him. We were infatuated with each other and I truly enjoyed his company. I saw him as limited, and at the same time skillful. He clearly loved women, but not up close. He loved them from a distance. His idea of a good life was to be involved with one woman at a time, for months, even years, and to keep his career at an even keel. He sort of controlled his environment by not reacting, instead he would forge ahead without any episodes.

> ## THE STOIC/OBJET D'ART AS INCOMMUNICADO
>
> He has never been taught to interpret signals
>
> He is misunderstood, which causes him to withdraw
>
> He appears unresponsive and cold because he is undeveloped
>
> He avoids social activities which might ovestimulate him
>
> His world is simplified and void of sensitivity

"There were no dramas in his life, it was an orderly and quiet world. Often we stayed at home. We were together like this for three years. It was a background story, and we did not go out into the world as much as we stayed in and had a private life together. He liked to have things his way, and it was a good relationship because I never resisted. He was strong and quiet and sure of himself because he had a narrow perspective. This worked for me at that stage in my life. Today I would want more. I knew instinctively that he was not going to offer more, that he was not capable of it. With my realization there came great freedom. At first I kept pushing and then I let it go—I sat back and said to myself, this is who he is, and it's fine for now."

YOU AS THE COMPROMISER

He expects you to do it his way. Your way is not part of the equation. He cannot recognize that you are compromising. Without the compromise, the relationship does not exist.

Coty's relationship with Dustin has been successful because she has not expected more from her stoic/objet d'art man than he is able to give. "I am very independent and I think that this drives Dustin to distraction. However, he is also relieved that he does not have to provide me with constant entertainment and offer hours of his time. I doubt that he could do it, if it was a requirement of mine. He likes to see that everyone around him is happy, and still he isn't really a part of any group. I am very social and he dislikes it. He wants ownership of me and this is not acceptable. We talk about it a lot. There are things that we do love to do together, sports and cooking. But there are things that we do apart. He is a loner and I'm so much a part of a crowd. This is a problem, but I've explained that I do not want to deny who I am for his sake. We are trying at present to find a balance that works.

"I see Dustin as very hardworking and decent, but not involved in life. It isn't as if he is a bystander who yearns to be a part of the world he watches. In fact, he is comfortable with his position. This way he never has to really feel. Despite that he doesn't seem to feel, I am convinced that he loves me and needs me. He would never discuss it on those terms, and I have come to these conclusions for myself. I'm fortunate that I'm confident enough to do it, because without my own sense of how Calvin feels, there'd be nothing. I know that I carry the emotional weight of the entire relationship. In return I get a man who is there to weather any storm and will not break down."

_____ Susan R. Shapiro and Michele Kasson, Ph.D.
CAN YOU AROUSE REAL FEELINGS?

There are limits to his abilities and limits to yours. If you are determined, you will overlook his actions and see beneath the surface. There stands the man who wants desperately to connect with you. Work and order are very important to him. You, as the objet d'art, will evoke the greatest reaction of all in a man who does not react. His defenses get in the way. He will defend against intimacy—it is your job to take him past it, knowing that you will never reach him deeply.

Ellen and Jess dated for one year before they married. Two years later, Ellen remembers how hard she worked to break down the barriers. "Jess could not converse. He was on all the time, he would tell jokes and make people laugh, but he could not really communicate. I could not get past his veneer for months and months. My friends would ask me what I saw in this guy. I suppose that I was attracted to his mask, to his way of never cracking, of never breaking down. We had worked together at a large corporation. I was in sales and he was one of the brains I would approach whenever I needed information. I realized early on that this man would not take any garbage from anyone. I knew that he disliked confrontation and would slip away instead of having a heart to heart. I also knew that I wanted him. So I approached him somewhat differently than I might have someone else. I was careful not to get in his way and to let him be the boss. I suppose it sounds very antiquated and deliberate, but there was something about him that appealed to me and also let me see inside the person. The insight that I gleaned I used wisely.

"The sex from the start was quite routine, almost rote. This was distressing. I knew that Jess was the most difficult man that I'd ever been with on many levels. Maybe it was a challenge, maybe it was timing. Timing has so much to do with how these situations turn out. But I was ready for him, and I knew what I was getting myself into. I told him in terms of the sex that I wanted him to hold me and to tell me how it felt to be with me. He thought I was crazy, but he tried. It was very difficult for him. We did get past some of the tense, distant times in our relationship—I would say that we are closer today than before. Yet Jess's basic nature remains and there is not a thing to do about it. I have decided it is okay if our sex is a physical need, not an intimacy. I have decided that it is acceptable to me that there are empty spaces in our relationship. I have truly decided on Jess and so I accept him and harbor a secret desire to walk him slowly, taking baby steps, toward a better path."

> **ROMANCE IS NOT HIS STRONG POINT**
> *He is not stupid, so teach him*
> *Do not beg for closeness*
> *Do not back off*
> *Work with his style*
> *Show support when he exhibits feelings*
> *Pick and choose your battles wisely*

HOW TO WIN HIM OVER

If you are a woman who defies the odds, a compromise might sate you. There are methods that will affect him, such as watching a movie, then discussing the emotions and conflict. If he takes you for granted and you feel as if he is absent, you can show him what matters. For example, if you want him to remember a birthday, he needs to be prompted and taught. But it is possible. Remember, this man will always prefer to be alone and it may be lonely to be at his side. He will always fear rejection at the same time that he craves closeness. He can self destruct by the height of the walls he has built around himself. A woman may be used by this man—for validation, to

_____ Susan R. Shapiro and Michele Kasson, Ph.D.

show off to the world. If you wait forever with this type, you will never get there. He is not easy to land, but it is not an impossible task.

10

*"Marriage, if one will face the truth, is an evil,
but a necessary evil."*
— Menander

THE MARRIED MAN

None of us has escaped hearing the tortured tale of a friend who takes up with a married man. There is no surcease from the angst and misery of listening to him swear from Labor Day through New Years Day, year in, year out, that he fully intends to leave his wife and children for you. He cannot live without you and you make his life palatable and bearable. She is a function for him, and nothing more. There is no passion, no real sex (unless he has a strong physical need), no real communication. If it wasn't for those glorious children, (at this moment, he whips out the latest photo and you notice that she is right there, smiling a toothy grin), he'd have left long ago. You have to be patient, he cannot destroy his canvas—be it the new house, the new job, the five year old's birthday party, but someday he will. You are patient and trusting, and finally angry and hostile.

_____ Susan R. Shapiro and Michele Kasson, Ph.D.

In Terry McMillan's novel, and film, *Waiting to Exhale*, there is a marvelous scene in which Whitney Houston's character tells her married lover that she no longer wants the relationship, astounding him by her sudden change of heart. It may be that her abrupt veer to the left is the only method that works in leaving one's married man. These relationships may go on for years, with the promises unending and the pain unbearable. According to statistics, one man in three has had an extramarital affair. There seems to be little correlation between the affair and the marriage for these men and thus the affair is kept at arms length. It is not viewed as a threat to the marriage or family. Yet the man who seeks out a lover while married is not content at home and will use the affair to fill the void. While it may take him years to leave his marriage, he bides his time with a lover to enhance his life.

We all remember what Jimmy Carter said in his notorious interview about lusting in his heart. The married man who takes a lover and remains in the marriage does not lust only in his heart, but breaks the rules in order to suit his needs. He is looking for sex, and intimate female friendship, and a safe haven. To the outer world he appears competent and in control, yet he needs solace somewhere and the other woman provides this.

UNHAPPY HUSBANDS

In deciding to lead a double life of the long standing affair, the married man is controlling more than one world. He controls two, that of his wife and children, and that of his lover. The affair is a chance to relive his youth and exert his male power.

For the modern woman who believes in her self-sufficiency, who is schooled and independent, there is little reason, at first, to shy away from the affair. After all, she rules her own life, she may choose whomever she wants. She believes that she is in charge of the situation. But this thinking often fails, and she becomes immersed in her affair without the emotional supports usually supplied by those closest to her. She cannot really confide in friends, because the affair is a secret. She has to live with social stigma and uncertainty, while her married man maintains both his fantasy life and his home life.

There are all sorts of married men who seek out lovers. There are those who do it quite unexpectedly, shaking the very essence of their perfectly ordered lives. The incredible high of the affair brings him to life, and boosts his self-esteem. What he cannot have with his wife, he will complement with his lover. If sex is lacking from the marriage, then the affair brings fabulous sex. If companionship is the missing ingredient, he seeks out a soul mate. *The marriage begins to lack a seductive quality. A comfort level settles in and the romance fades. If passion is not sparked on occasion, boredom will replace it, providing fertile ground for an affair to flourish.*

> **DEMANDS OF MARRIAGE**
> *Children, work and bills*
> *A household to run*
> *An unsexual partner who was once sexual*
> *The drudgery of day to day living*

While fidelity is considered intrinsic to retaining the sacred quality of marriage, the married men out there are ready and willing to go for the affair. And women are autonomous—be it the workplace or by employing day care, there are means to make the hours to have a secret liason. Unlike the past where intimate relationships did not exist until a marriage, most married people today have had a variety of experiences beforehand. For these players, there is the known quantity of sexual freedom. The married man who has a lover is more accustomed to the drill—

_____ Susan R. Shapiro and Michele Kasson, Ph.D.

he is only adding one more color to his palate. The marriage vows are of minor concern.

> **M.O. OF THE MARRIED MAN**
> *He tells you how exciting you are*
> *The sex is unending*
> *He pays for everything*
> *He is gallant and loving*
> *His wife does not understand him*
> *He begs you to give him time*

We think of illustrious men who have had affairs—Burt Reynolds was known for this, as was Woody Allen, with his lover, Mia Farrow's adopted daughter. Donald Trump and Marla Maples, who became his second wife, made quite a splash when their union was first announced. King Henry VIII, the most infamous of all, actually shook a country to its roots politically and religiously in order to divorce his wife and marry his mistress. More recent, and most prominent of all married men is Prince Charles, who publicly announced his insatiable love for a woman other than his wife.

In some cases these affairs have become a catalyst to leave the marriage, *although not necessarily for the lover.* Does the married man simply replace one relationship with another? In the case of many a married man, he does not leave the marriage, and may not even speak of leaving, but leads the other woman on by sustaining the affair. If you hang onto your married man, believing that one day he will leave her for you, it likely is a dead end. The married man who has been married for many years may stray and yet return to the marriage, renewed.

Elyssa's married man was unencumbered, having only a wife to deal with and no children. When they met at a bus depot on a Saturday morning, Elyssa had no knowledge that Derek was even married. "He did not wear a wedding ring, nor did he mention the fact that he had a wife who he was traveling home to see. Instead we spoke of our careers and of our interests. I was absolutely bowled over—I had not met anyone like Derek. And at thirty-five, I'd been dating for years. So when we both returned to Connecticut, he called me and asked me out to lunch. I had had so many first dates that were lunches that I thought nothing of it. It wasn't until much later, say five dates later, that he confessed. I was devastated. But I was also relieved when he said there were no children in the picture. We proceeded to have a long standing affair. I would travel to meet him. He would make excuses to his wife and spend the afternoons in a hotel room with me. Then I'd travel home, alone and bereft. I really couldn't stand the set up, but I made the conscious effort to wait it out. I knew in my heart of hearts that he loved me and that he was very unhappy in his marriage. I believed that he would be strong enough to leave some day.

"This affair with Derek went on for years. I shudder to think of how many weekends we sneaked around, and during the week as well. Finally, after five years, Derek decided to get divorced. One day he came to me and announced that he was ready and that he had told her. For all of my closest friends and my mother suggesting that I give him an ultimatum, I never had. And it paid off. Because had I pressured him, we would not have succeeded. Today we are married, happily, with two young daughters. While I don't recommend that any woman get herself entangled with a married man, my story ended on a positive note. But during the years when it was an affair, there was enormous pain and sadness. A sense of futility hung over us. I would refuse to acknowledge the wife's existence. Had I given that my energy, I would have been devastated."

_____ Susan R. Shapiro and Michele Kasson, Ph.D.
AN AFFAIR AS A BOOSTER

> *The affair gives the married man's life new meaning. For years he has been asleep, going through the motions. He is a good father and good provider but there is no inspiration in the marriage. You, as the lover, provide this for him. You are his wake up call. Unfortunately, in many cases, he wakes up to have his cake and eat it too.*

For the married man in mid-life, there is the possibility that he is attracted to a younger woman, a newer model, a method of keeping him young. If he trades in his first wife for a younger version, he may perpetuate a period of his life when he felt most virile and fit—as a father of young children, with a young wife. If the married man is concerned about growing older, a woman who is substantially younger is a means of not facing it. On the other hand, he might not want to be with someone who is younger because the contrast is too great and he will feel only older by comparison.

Lifestyle contributes to the rise in extramarital affairs. The dynamic of the workplace is conducive, with late hours and young women climbing the corporate ladder at a rapid rate. There is a titilation to working on a project into the dawn, and the coworkers become confidantes. One thing leads to another.

THE WIFE
She tries to keep the marriage together

The infidelity is an invisible weight

To lose him is often to lose her home and finances

She hangs onto the ideal, although she is emotionally bereft

The affair exists because of an unhappiness in the marriage

THE OTHER WOMAN
She offers him a private universe

She is an aphrodisiac, there is secrecy and longing

She is willing, for a while, to put up with the constraints

She is chosen, the wife is a given

Shelley had known Julius for several years through business before they embarked on an extramarital affair. At the time that it began, Shelley had a young son and was pregnant with her second child. Julius had been married for two years and had no children. "I never planned to get involved with someone while I was married. It is against my morals and everything that I believe in. But I was very unhappily married and I think that Julius was also. My marriage was lonely and he described his in a similar way. I suppose that I was attracted to Julius from the moment that he came into my office. We were assigned several projects and had to work closely together. Eventually we became lovers. I was pregnant, which sounds really strange. My husband was not interested in me sexually during the pregnancy and this was part of his 'madonna syndrome'. Either I was pregnant and untouchable or I wasn't pregnant, but rejected because I was the mother of his children. It didn't matter, I was no longer enticing to him. I truly missed the sexual part of the marriage and Julius was a wonderful lover. He made me feel alive again, and sexual.

"It was like being reborn. We definitely fell for one another. He told me that he would leave his wife and take care of my babies. I know that he meant it, but he had less at stake than I did. I could not tear my family apart, and so after months and months of agony, we parted. But Julius is

> **WHO DOES THE MARRIED MAN CHOOSE?**
> *She has low self-esteem and is willing to share his fantasy world*
> *She is afraid of commitment*
> *She can handle a sexual relationship*
> *She has been seriously injured in the past*
> *She may be young, just wetting her toes in the workplace*
> *She does not want to compete for the available men*

_____ Susan R. Shapiro and Michele Kasson, Ph.D.

never far from my mind. He came to visit me in the hospital when my son was born, in the guise of a friend from work. And we would meet in the park with my children once in a while. I saw that he would be a good father, and I know that he is a good man. Although he is married, his marriage is like a relationship, because there are no ties. In my case, there is lots of baggage, say two babies. I understand how lonely both of us are in our marriages. His is particularly miserable because his wife is not sympathetic. Or so I believe. I suppose we each have married the wrong person. And I will remain married due to circumstances. The price I pay is missing Julius terribly and the life we might have had together."

PASSIONATE LIAISONS

The married man transfers his passion to his lover. She becomes the recipient of his gifts, thoughts and plans. Yet she does not actually have him, it is an illusion. These feelings have super mileage, and keep the affair going.

When a married man leaves a marriage, there is often the residue and memory of the first marriage which gets in the way of the second. Regardless of his desire to leave and his initiating a divorce, he may be conflicted when he is actually divorced. There are married men who are able to project this scenario and avoid it by remaining in their marriage. Their rationale is always the children and lifestyle and the promise made to their wives. They will cheat both the lover and the wife, as well as themselves of a whole life by continuing the affair and staying in the marriage. No one has this man totally, but everyone gets snippets. It is an unfortunate, no win situation. The married man who has an affair is truly denying those who love him the opportunity for a full life.

The Men Out There

THE STEREOTYPIC AFFAIR

This man has a wife who withholds sex and a mistress who makes amazing love. Sex is not the entire story—it is one aspect of the relationship. Their very secret is their bond. There are shared confidences and no outer world to infringe upon them. The time constraints make each moment a stolen one. They have the facade of eternal romance. Erotic love has nothing to do with children and mortgage payments.

Romantic love has always been idealized in our society and in ancient times. Mystifying and compelling, in certain European societies, adultery was the norm. In Europe, adultery provided satisfying love, sex and companionship. The affair, for the married man, provides a relief from the day to day drudgery of life. It evokes intense feelings of affection and desire. Yet the married man who remains married creates a triangular situation, whereby the lover and wife and he are united, whether it be conscious or not. The adventure of the affair is juxtaposed with the ordinary stability of marriage. Divorce, which is equivalent to a death, might be put off by an affair. The married man who is satisfied by two women, not one, will not need to initiate a divorce.

Helene and her married man, Bernie, have been having an illicit affair for over a year. While Bernie has made noises that he wants to leave his ten year old marriage, Helene no longer believes him. "I wish that he would not make those lukewarm promises. I wish that he would be up front with me and admit that the affair is the icing on his cake. It's been a strange setup because we live in the same apartment building and I have to be very discreet. Sometimes I see his wife in the elevator or doing errands in the neighborhood. I watch her with their three children with a sick feeling in my stomach. I really do not want to be a home wrecker but I remind myself that I can't break what isn't breakable. I can see her side of it, how she must wonder where he is some of the time and how it must feel to be in the dark, but not really.

"She has to know, in the deepest corners of her mind that he spends time with someone else. He comes to my apartment and we have meals together and share secrets. The sex is unbelievable. The very idea that he goes back to her, to their bedroom is nauseating. He is a fun loving man and someone to care so deeply for. I know that we could have a wonderful life together. It is his children that worry me. That is why I will never encourage him to leave. How can I, when it is about not just his life, but all of theirs? Somehow I worry about his wife less, she will find someone else. We all do. Does that mean I should find someone else when I love Bernie? I know that being his lover is not moral, but I truly love him. It is a real love affair and he is a good man. We are absolutely in love and tortured. I tell him that I understand. I do not want to hang around forever, listening to what he relishes with me but can't do anything about. It is too hurtful."

> **FALSE PROMISES**
>
> *Your sex is the only sex that counts*
>
> *He cannot live without your secret meetings*
>
> *As soon as the first kid is in junior high he'll leave*
>
> *As soon as the second kid is in junior high he'll leave*
>
> *He never has oral sex with his wife, only you*
>
> *He has less sex with her because of you*
>
> *Family outings are misery because of you*

The woman who is in love with a married man can make excuses at every turn. She blames his wife and his work, his hectic schedule for his harried state. The desperation of the single woman who connects with this man is partly due to statistics. There are more single women than single men in certain echelons. In the work force there is the educated single woman in mid-life who attends a convention filled with unhappily married mid-life men. It is ripe turf for the beginnings of an affair. Of course the married man who can be readily influenced by a woman, an outsider, may meet her under any circumstance. *If he tells her that he would never be in such a situation had he not met her, do not believe him. In fact the affair is all about him and what his needs are.*

Jan stopped dating Maurice soon after he revealed his living situation. Although she met him at a singles dinner club, she began to feel that he was not forthcoming about his situation. "I really liked this guy and wanted to go out with him. He was kind of shy and alluring at the same time. He seemed very vulnerable. He said that he was separated from his wife and child. I learned that he was not separated and lived at home still. He claimed there was no marriage and that he was moving toward a divorce. I know that he had all of the machinations of a marriage, that it appeared intact to me. Our schedule further convinced me of this. So we began to have an affair, that's really what it was. But I made it brief because I didn't want to be the other woman. I told him when he served papers I'd be ready to date. A woman would have to be pretty naive to take his story on face value.

WHO TEMPTS HIM

A risk taking woman who is used to winning will seek out a married man for the sport. A woman who does not want a committed relationship has the perfect excuse in her married man. The woman who absolutely falls in love with a married man and wants a total life will also seek him out, but will suffer tremendously. The woman who is needy and believes his transparent lies is irresistible to him.

_____ Susan R. Shapiro and Michele Kasson, Ph.D.

When Betina met Hank at a New Years Eve brunch, she hadn't a clue that he was married. He presented himself as a single man looking for a relationship and had dated several of Betina's acquaintances, in a peripheral manner. "I thought that he was handsome and charming and that I'd finally met someone who sparked some interest for me. We would go for lunch frequently during the week and to dinner on the same day on occasion. He had a high powered job and traveled extensively. Sometimes I traveled with him and that was wonderful. After six months of seeing Hank exclusively I confronted him with my concern that we never spent any time together on the weekends. I could no longer believe his excuses about work and I began to suspect there was someone else. What I wasn't prepared for was the truth, that he had two children and a wife in the very same town. I was bowled over and devastated. I had begun to fall for him big time. I told him I would not be second fiddle to his obligations to his family. It was different when I did not know. He had presented himself to a community as a single man which meant that he was a total liar and had no intention of revealing the truth. It was only by accident that I learned the facts."

Betina was unwilling to pretend that being second place was acceptable, which many women in her situation will do. Nor did she believe that he would give up his wife for her in the future. What most commonly occurs in the case of the married man is that the lover must give up part of herself and always listen to his story without ever expressing herself. She cannot demand that he leave and think that it will happen. She knows better and usually subjugates her needs for his. Most married men do not leave their wives and children for their lover. Instead they hope to keep the affair going. This can last for years on end.

IF A MARRIED MAN DOES LEAVE FOR YOU

The married man is often with the lover because it is a fantasy world for him. He is not willing to grow in the relationship with his wife so he searches for the high points with someone else. If he actually leaves the wife for the lover, he is looking for the continuation of the fantasy life. But fantasy is no longer possible when the mundane sets in. Frequently the married man does not survive this rude awakening with his catalyst/lover and finds someone else to fulfill his dreams.

Ironically, the married man can be one who does not wish to be committed. Similar to the commitment phobic man, he will avoid attachment. If he wasn't attached previously, it is not likely that he can become truly attached in the future. For example, the unconnected man who marries and believes that he is "settling down" is really creating his own hell. He is not someone who can handle this lifestyle, and deludes himself. He may crave it as he rejects it. What works in this self-fulfilling trap he has set is to find a lover. Then he no longer feels he is married, it is an illusion of freedom. The monogamy that dictated the beginnings of the marriage does not seem all encompassing anymore. The main relationship, that with his wife, now becomes a misery. He finds fault with her however and whenever he can.

Alfred and Virginia were married for six years when Alfred took up with Margie. Although Margie knew he was married and accepted his terms of the affair, her secret hope was that she could win him over. Virginia, like Margie, had had such designs on Alfred only seven years before when she had disengaged him from a live-in relationship. According to Margie, Virginia tortured Alfred while she was the source of comfort and joy for him. "I did not feel like a home wrecker because there was great discontent long before I came into the picture. Virginia would have been the first to admit this. But when she found out about us, she came to my office and went ballistic. She knew that I was serious about him, having found a telephone bill. I suspect that Alfred had done this on purpose, to let her know. It was a cheap shot and she was livid.

"I resented that he dragged me into it, instead of being strong enough to simply leave or to decide against the affair. I realized how weak Alfred was when I listened to Virginia's story of his past. Apparently she had been as determined as I was to win him over and to conform him. But he has a missing piece of morality and cannot really do the right thing without causing everyone around him a terrific amount of pain. He allows himself to be influenced by whoever is the stronger woman. In this case, it became me. Virginia was the stronger woman the last time and she ended up his wife. Then I became the stronger woman and he was setting me up too. This was too much for me and I bolted. I actually empathized with Virginia. I began to see how it was for his partner. I knew that if he had done this to Virginia, I was next."

The married man is exciting because he is unattainable. The women who like this at the outset grow very weary of it over time. What has thrills and chills at the start, loses its appeal as the married man reveals himself. He will say that he cannot meet you when his wife is away for more than several hours because he is in charge

> **WOE BE THE LOVER AND THE WIFE**
> The triangle is his creation
> He complains bitterly about the marriage
> You believe his tales
> To leave the marriage, he must find fault with his wife
> If you become the primary relationship, he no longer sees you as flawless

of the dog and the hamster. He will tell you that he is misunderstood at home, the most classic of tales, and has only you to appreciate him. In the same breath he will tell you that the trip he had to take to the Caribbean was not all bad and that his wife is an excellent wind surfer. You are always quiet and unhappy. You hang on to his phone calls and weep on Saturday night. In a love affair, one of the heart, the conclusion that love is not enough is difficult to face.

WHY ARE YOU THERE?

There are several psychological theories that contribute to the reason why a single woman would want to be in this place. One states that she is in search of the father she could never attain. Another is her need to punish herself. Theory or not, she is most likely positioning herself for heartbreak. There is a small percentage of winners in this drama. The arms of the married man are ultimately dangerous.

Janine and Michael met ten summers ago on vacation. Both avid sailors, they found themselves at their boats at the same marina each morning. Janine knew that Michael was married and watched him closely with his two young daughters. "I observed the whole family and I was intrigued. I thought that his wife was a good mother and that he was a devoted father. The girls were adorable. I rarely saw him with his wife, usually with the children. And she did not seem so happy to be sailing every morning. One day he came to the boat alone and we began to talk. He confided in me immediately that he was not content and had not been from the start. I believed him but I wondered why he was in a marriage with children if he'd known all along. We began to see each other in the city after the summer and I definitely fell for him. Michael returned the affection.

"It was a dilemma for him. I told him after ten months of sneaking around and my eating candy bars alone on weekends that I wanted him to make a decision. Michael told me that his children were too young. I said I couldn't wait, I wanted to have children of my own. I told him to step up to the plate or find another game. He left his wife and divorced her within a year. We were married as soon as possible. I plunged ahead, and was pregnant within fifteen months of the wedding.

"In retrospect, with three children of our own today, and his ex-wife remarried, I see that it is all attainable but there is a big penalty. Michael has enormous guilt for his behavior and his two daughters, now older, are resentful of me and of the second family. I would not recommend that anyone go for a man who is married with children and think they can get away clean. It is a fraught and guilt ridden situation. Michael's real mistake was staying married to her at all, and having those babies with her. He made his own trap and then could never quite escape it. I had the feeling on many nights at the beginning that he mourned for the life he had left behind."

THE RELUCTANT MARRIED MAN

He has been pushed into this marriage and has felt compromised from the start. He concentrates on other aspects of life, such as his career or sports or friendships because he is lonely in the marriage. He adores his children and gives them love but his wife is left wanting. His wife will take care of him because he seems needy. He does not rock the boat. His wife might be a more powerful figure who tells him what to do.

Andrea and her married man, Arthur, have been together for over five years. Despite Arthur's repeated promises to leave his unhappy situation, Andrea has had no hard evidence that this will happen. "I have listened to every story Arthur has shared about his marriage. What I don't understand is why he complains so about the marriage and is frozen there. He simply can't help himself. I have been seeing him three times a week for all these years, and I have been told repeatedly that it is only a matter of time before he leaves. He tells me how he can't be without me, how his life is incomplete if I'm not there. He never wanted to be married to his wife, it was something he felt pushed into. She is very strong, and very sure of herself. Doesn't she have a clue? Doesn't she know that she's getting bits and pieces? And I'm beginning to wonder about Arthur. Who is he to inflict this on both of us? For every year that goes by, she gets older and neither of us really have him, so we have nothing. I am waiting to see, but I'm putting a cap on this. If in six months time we are not any further along, I will leave this and get on with my life."

THE RISKS ARE OBVIOUS

The woman who likes histrionics and has a competitive spirit will pursue the married man. The ego experiences the high of the game, and this propels her forward. The idea of never expressing her own needs fully does not deter her. The secret realm of the affair is enough for her. No matter how it ends, she has had him like no one else has.

In a society where marriage is not considered a permanent state, the married man and his lover may view themselves as blameless, as a product of circumstance. With marriage and coupling no longer considered a necessity, people want romance and love. Today, the idea of men at work and women at home is not approached as the norm. While the other woman may feel some guilt and a definite jealousy toward the wife, she will also deny her culpability.

_____ Susan R. Shapiro and Michele Kasson, Ph.D.

The marriage does not seem a real relationship to the other woman, and anything that transpires between the married man and his wife is less than significant. If they go on vacation together, the other woman writhes in pain at home, promising herself that he's having a horrible time. When he sleeps with his wife, she understands that he has to placate her and that it doesn't really count. The marriage is much less real than the affair, the other woman promises herself. *And so she waits, becoming more and more isolated, dependent upon her married man and unfulfilled in the process.*

Krissy met Bob at an elementary school where both were working. Bob had been married for six years and had a newborn daughter at home. Krissy was in graduate school and had just left a long standing relationship. "The attraction was instantaneous—electrifying. I was so attracted to Bob. I kept my distance because I knew that he was married and had a baby. But we couldn't really keep away from one another and we began an affair that has lasted for three years. It's been filled with highs and lows, but mostly I have been very lonely and frustrated.

"I have gone out with several available men, but I'm in love with Bob. I cannot ask him to leave his wife when he has this small child. It is completely his decision. I know that he loves me, but I suspect that he loves his wife too. I think of her, she is this presence in my life. Until about a month ago, I had kept very quiet. Then I met someone at a family party. We have begun to date and I am happy and healthy for the first time in years. When I told Bob about it, he told me he would leave the marriage. Then he told his wife about us. This puts him in a terrible position, whether he leaves or stays. I am inclined to simply walk now. Not because there are any guarantees elsewhere. On the other hand, I suffered for years.

"I see having an affair with a married man as a no win

situation no matter what the outcome is. Today I wait to see if he will leave or not. And the timing is ironic, now that I have finally found another life for myself. My advice to any woman who falls for a married man is, run the other way and never look back."

IF YOU MUST PURSUE HIM

He might keep you hanging on for years. He will be consumed with remorse if he leaves for you. Trust is a big issue for the relationship, having cheated once, he may do so again. You will have a great enemy in the ex-wife and perhaps in the children if he does divorce for your sake.

IT WORKS BOTH WAYS

As the wife one must pay attention to her husband's needs. If she can sustain his interest in the marriage, he will not stray. As the lover, one must understand the consequences. The odds are that your married man will want both you and his marriage.

There are always the cases of the unhappily married couple. Both partners in this predicament employ their own means of escape, be it submerging oneself in work or charity, the children or perhaps athletics. The married man who yearns to get out of his marriage may use the affair as a means to do so. He will take up with another woman and then lie to his wife when she becomes suspicious. He will leave evidence for her in the hope that she will confront him. He may then react in one of several ways, but frequently will admit that he has been less than pleased for a long period of time. It is now a relief for him because he no longer has to carry the weight of his secret. He is liberated in the sense that he does not have to pretend anymore. For the duration of the affair, he has had to feign that the marriage is not a marriage, that the commitment he made to his wife is not significant. It is almost as if the affair has enabled him to let go of the marriage. Thus you, as the other woman, are his spring board to freedom. And while the affair was in the beginning stages, you, as the lover, offered him the illusion of being a free agent. *The married man is in a triangle from day one. Only when he makes a clean break, for or against the marriage, is he true to himself. Remember, until then, you are the victim of his circumstances and his needs.*

> ## HOW TO MAKE IT WORK AS THE LOVER
> *State your needs early on*
> *Do not enable him to have two lives*
> *Love him enough to lure him*
> *Do not remain if he is not forthcoming*
>
> ## HOW TO MAKE IT WORK AS THE WIFE
> *Do not let the sex slide*
> *Give attention to him as well as to the children*
> *Create your own life*
> *Make time to be together and enjoy one another's company*
> *Do not accept his absences*

11

"So in the morning, don't say you love me 'cause you know I'll only kick you out the door."
— Rod Stewart

SEX/THE CONNECTION

While there can be sex without love and love without sex, it is really the combination of the two that works in a successful and complete relationship. When there is an intimate connection, sex is the expression of the intimacy, it is a closeness that enriches both partners and makes them feel wonderful. On the one hand, there is sex for sport as seen in Champion Sport/Macho Man, or there is love without a fulfilling sexual component. In a situation where the sex is not viable, there is a missing piece and a longing for what does not happen. The ideal is to find the balance between the two. One never feels more alive than when her pheromones are at their peak and her partner is the recipient. However, one is never more disappointed than when she meets a man who is fabulous and the chemistry doesn't click.

Each of us has experienced the man who gives good

phone. He is humorous, happy, charming, intelligent, and similar to you in his likes and interests. It's too good to be true, and when you meet, you know that for a fact. Or he sounds like he's a winner and at first glance you cannot keep your hands off each other. The two of you begin to date at a rapid pace. There is a glow when you enter a room and his phone calls are golden. You finally go to bed together and fall into each other's arms. It is everything that you dreamed it would be and more. *You have achieved the ideal situation, until you realize the relationship is about lust, not love. Once more you are tossed into the sea of uncertainty. Lust cannot sustain a long term commitment.*

There are those women who exemplify a freedom of choice in their men and the lives they share together. For instance, Georgia O'Keefe, the artist, had a penchant for younger men as she grew older. Erica Jong has repeatedly written about the independence of women who know the importance of sex in a relationship. Madonna is the quintessential sex icon who has made her view apparent to her public. In everyday life, sexual intimacy *and* emotional stability are the goal.

Laurie, at the age of forty-seven, has become seriously involved with a man eighteen years her junior. Tai and she met in race driving school. For Laurie, there is a recurring disappointment in Tai's lack of desire. "At first I thought he had a low libido because he didn't want to sleep with me. Now I realize that he does not want me in that way. But it seems he might be changing his mind. It's a case of if you think you can have it, you don't want it. We have discussed this and I have told him that I want him to use me to find his own sexuality. I am his human sacrifice. He loves me and trusts me, and we are totally connected except for the sex. He is conflicted because I am older. Although we live together, I believe that he sleeps with younger women when

I am at work. Everything is absolutely wonderful, except for the sex. He loves me to death and constantly talks about the love he feels. When someone loves you for your inner self, you still want there to be more.

"Tai provides me with wonderful words, flowers, tapes, music. He serenades me, and offers everything but sex. When we have had sex, he stops short. He kisses me, but that's it. I am convinced that age is the deterrent, that it is circumstantial, and that there is a natural progression. Today he loves me but does not desire me physically. I no longer believe I am desirable because he rejects me. It's the ultimate challenge. I have created my own reality. My only fear was that I would no longer be young and attractive. Now I am with someone who gives me that very message."

> **DOES SEX RULE THE DAY?**
> Are you unhappy with him when you are not in bed?
> Are your fantasies of him only sexual?
> Do your conversations focus on sexual innuendo?
> Has your reading material become a Victoria's Secret catalog?
> Do you spend your dates eating Chinese food in bed?

Laurie's preoccupation with immortality and sexual persona has driven her to choose an unsuitable partner who undermines her sexuality. She has sabotaged her own happiness by choosing inappropriately. However, most of us avoid such self-defeating situations.

For instance, sexual chemistry was a big part of Belle's and Walt's relationship. At a class dinner for second graders, they were seated together as the only single parents at the event. A month later when he called her, Belle could not recall Walt. "It was because I was in a dry spell that I accepted the date. I didn't remember much about him, and he seemed to remember me in detail. He is not my type physically at all, he is too tall and heavy set for my taste. I'm thin and wiry and usually attracted to someone more my size. On our first date I found him seductive and he had a great technique for relating to me. There wasn't much intimacy so it was fine. He wasn't what I wanted, not in terms of career or his looks or his way of relating to others. He wasn't intimate with me in a way I wanted him to be. I could not discuss things with him, he was gruff and not accessible. But when we made love, it was like nothing I had ever experienced in my entire life. Although our children remained in the background, I was willing to discuss living together based on the sex. It was such a draw for me that I actually considered it. I have never in my life had such a priority. I knew that he wasn't for me but I was unable to leave because of the sex.

"The relationship did not survive because it wasn't based on a friendship. In fact, we argued so about whether I could bring my animals to his place, if we were to live together, that it began to unravel. He sent me a letter saying that he was not only allergic to animals but listed all of my negative qualities. I was so relieved to have this in my hands, and to face the fact that sex is not enough. This man was not for me in any way, from the beginning."

If a woman has not had a sexual relationship that is all encompassing, it is a wake up call for her. Often she will mistake the sexual feeling for an emotional response and will suffer the consequences. It is only when the sex is a result of the emotions that it truly sustains the relationship. One needs to take time to realize how the relationship grows and the sex along with it. It can't be rushed, or the sex may become the entire relationship and the potential for deep friendship and true intimacy become nonexistent. In a mature situation, the two are parallel, the emotional and physical grow alongside. Because women surrender themselves, it is a double edged sword. *If a woman surrenders under the right conditions, she is giving herself to the man who wants her. If she surrenders under the wrong conditions, she is giving away her soul.* Because so many women feel that they belong to a man by becoming his lover, it is a tricky proposition.

THE CULTURAL DOUBLE STANDARD

It is acceptable for men to want women only for sex but not acceptable for women to want men only for sex. Men are stimulated visually, women need to provide a level of sexuality. A flannel nightgown and sweat stocks do not suffice when your man is out in the world with sexy young women all day. It is up to the woman after she has become comfortable sexually to remember to be seductive in the bedroom. Long term commitments run the risk of sexual boredom and women must remember to keep their sensuality alive.

Our emotions play a large part in our sexuality. Our ability to experience sexual satisfaction is as much a matter of our minds as our bodies. For both males and females, sexual functioning is an arena for expressing fears and anxieties. Men in particular are subject to anxieties concerning their sexual performance. Our society places much emphasis on the male anatomy and its functioning. Performance anxiety is a result of a man's fear concerning his ability to perform sexually. The women who men meet today are not fresh out of their parents' home. They have sexual sophistication and awareness, and are not naive about their sexuality. A man's fears about a woman's expectations can play a forceful role in a budding relationship.

SEX AS A WEAPON
You no longer feel like pleasing each other
He withholds sex and you feel rejected
You withhold sex and he's irate
He leaves for sex elsewhere
You take on a lover

_____ Susan R. Shapiro and Michele Kasson, Ph.D.

Susie and Darryl have been together for two years. Susie, a real estate broker in her early forties and Darryl, an art teacher, met at the supermarket. Susie has two daughters, ages seven and nine, and Darryl has a son in college. Sparks were flying from the beginning and within weeks they were intimate. "I fell for Darryl absolutely. I was captivated by his dark hair and green eyes from the moment we met. I could tell by how he looked at me that he felt the same way. We started dating and it was very clear that something special was going on. We found that we had a lot to talk about but what we wanted to do was to kiss and touch all of the time. Then that first special night happened. I got myself all prepared with my favorite lingerie and perfume, knowing that we were going to be intimate. He had his place ready for me with soft music and lighting. It was perfect. I knew that it was going to be heaven just by his kisses on the last several dates. But then it was less than what I had expected. He knew it too, and we talked about it. Even though I hadn't known him for a very long time, we had always been very honest and intimate with each other. And we didn't say much, but I quietly reassured him that everything was okay. I knew that this wasn't what his sexuality was really like. I knew by everything about him.

"Darryl is a very self assured guy and he's also assured about his sexuality. He said that I threw him a little bit by being too forward for him. We tried again during that week and this time I did not rush him. I let him take the lead. And by the third time that we were together, he had become everything I had expected on the first night. It wasn't only the newness that had made him nervous at first, but because we had a real shot at being together that he felt anxious. Today we are extremely sexual and content. I know that our initial disappointment could have destroyed the entire relationship."

The Men Out There

WHEN IMPOTENCE STRIKES

In a situation where the man does not perform as he believes he ought to, the woman can become unhappy and insecure as a result. More serious difficulties may ensue. All men at some time in their lives will experience impotence. Illness, alcohol, medication and smoking are common causes. While the effect may be easy to remedy, if the man becomes unnerved by his experience, he may develop impotence based on feelings of his own adequacy.

Victoria, who lives in San Francisco, has been dating Sal for the past two years. Both are divorced and in their late thirties. Although Sal is impotent, Victoria feels it is some of the best sex she has ever experienced. "This man cannot come inside of me but has to jerk off. He gets hard but it does not last and he cannot sustain an erection. Everyone thinks that Sal is a real ladies man. Sometimes he makes me feel uneasy when we are alone together but when we go to a party or out in public, he is the life of the party. I know that as I become older, I become more assertive sexually. I tell him what I want and he listens. He has made me feel terrific sexually and I have gotten used to his problem. There have been some times when we have been together when it is not really enough for me, but usually it is fabulous. He won't get help and has never sought help. He tells me it is from a trauma. He has children and is divorced, so I assume he was able to at some point.

"We have fun together and are very close. We see each other two or three times a week. I will stay with him at his place but I wish that it could be more often. Some nights I will go over to his house just for the sex, late at night. I will wear great lingerie and I will be aching for him. I am in love with him but I doubt that he is in love with me. I want

Susan R. Shapiro and Michele Kasson, Ph.D.

> **HOW SERIOUS IS IMPOTENCE?**
>
> *Has it been a life long problem or is it new?*
> *Has he made changes in diet or medication?*
> *Is there anxiety at work or in the relationship?*
> *Has there been a major change in his life?*

him to yearn for me, but he doesn't. I think that sex is the hook here which I wish wasn't the case, but I have to face it. I have been willing to overlook the problem because of how he compensates and because I am so locked into him. I have changed over the years, I would never have been with a man with such a problem five years ago. I feel that there are worse things that can happen in a relationship and I am willing to stick with him. For me, the issue is that I want him badly enough to see him late at night. That is demeaning. But the impotence is not about that. The impotence I can accept, it is his treatment of me that I worry about."

Cecilia and Garrett were together for several months when the relationship showed signs of failure. Cecilia, childless at the age of forty, was quite hopeful that Garrett could be the one. "Garrett was a great guy. We had met as soon as I broke up with the man I was living with. I really didn't think that I could like somebody so quickly but he was very special. Our phone conversations lasted for hours even though he lived nearby. There was laughter and we shared a view of life. We had the same values. For this reason, I was very hopeful. When I slept with Garrett, he was tender and loving, experienced in anticipating my wants and knowing how to give me pleasure. But there was one thing lacking. Garrett could not maintain an erection. I never found out why but I know that he had been married once and that it had been a problem. When I look back, I wonder if I should have handled it differently. These doubts will remain with me always. But I was so unhappy with the problem that I couldn't stay with him. There were so many things about him that were perfect. But impotence was a very big deal to me."

Many women do not know how to handle impotence and are not schooled in what it is about. They may not understand that in many cases it is a temporary problem and one that is reactive. A woman may feel that this is a lifelong problem where there are no solutions, although for many men there are now several options. She may also feel that the impotence is a reflection of his desire for her. If a woman is educated, she will not feel hurt or as if it is a personal affront. Rather she may take a mature approach, where she is caring and loving and may be able to walk him through it. *When the man experiences impotence, unless the partners are true partners and are able to communicate, they will move away from each other, often in an unhappy silence.*

Tanya's relationship with Mac was influenced by his sexual dysfunction. After six months, they stopped seeing one another despite their compatibility on several levels. "He was my intellectual equal and I knew that he respected me. I respected him too. His work made sense to me and I was interested in hearing about his day. He treated me nicely and told me that I was exactly what he had been looking for. He was divorced with a child and at the age of forty-five, he was ready to make a second commitment. I was divorced with two children, and at the age of thirty-nine I knew that this could have worked. But the sex was such an obstacle for me that I really couldn't overlook it. The problem was that even though he was middle-aged, he was as knowledgeable about sex as a teenager. It felt as if he had grown up in a sexual vacuum, and I didn't want to be his teacher. He didn't know how to hold me, or kiss me, and he experienced premature ejaculation, also like a teenager. I guess that I could have hung in there, but it was so distasteful to me. The first time I thought he was anxious because it was new. After that, I was patient with him because I cared for him so much. He told me that sex was never a large part of his life. But as time went on, I didn't like the role of being the mentor, and feeling so unfilled myself. I started to fantasize about being with a hunk who would gather me up in his arms and overpower me. I knew then that it was over."

Many times when a woman is not receiving sexual contentment from her mate, she will avoid him sexually. If the relationship between the partners is not open and loving, most likely he will develop anxiety about his performance. His difficulties may be minor, but can become an impotence problem if he develops concerns about having intercourse.

WHAT ARE THE STEPS?

He needs to feel loved and accepted. Sexual problems will sap his confidence in the bedroom and beyond it. The first step is to be able to talk to him about your feelings and his. The second step is to seek some kind of aid to remedy the difficulty. Medical evaluation is a must if the problem becomes more serious. Once the cause of the difficulty is ascertained, a variety of treatment options become available.

Sharon and Ira worked for an international corporation and met when he was in town on business. They were both in their early forties, divorced with teenage children from their previous marriages. "I met Ira at a business dinner. We were flirting and chatting, but I really didn't pay much attention to him as a real possiblilty since he lived in Europe. A week later, I received a note from him in the mail and this was the beginning. His letters were very warm and similar in style to my own. It often looked as if I wrote them myself. They were funny and became more and more intimate. Ira became my spiritual partner. We began talking to each other frequently and developed a love which grew from a distance. I had no memory of what he looked like. I sent him a picture, included relevant statistics, and hoped that he would find me attractive since I am five years older than he. Then he came to town. There he was, cute, and alien to me. It took me a half hour to realize that this was the same person who knew all of my most secret thoughts for the last six months.

"Before long the relationship became physical as well as spiritual, emotional and intellectual. He had a problem with impotence, but I didn't. He really loves women, and women's bodies. He likes to be with women and enjoys them. He was generous and sensual. I knew that even though he had difficulty getting hard, he did have a previous sex life, and had children. We were so close in so many ways that we were able to talk about our sexuality in a loving manner. We read books on sensuality, and shared our learning both about men and women. We talked about going to a therapist and ultimately he was referred to a physician. Ira learned how to inject himself with papavin. It's been a solution for him. He becomes hard and is able to ejaculate, and then remains hard for a while longer. He feels as if he's gotten his manhood back, and we are both very satisfied with our physical relationship. The only issue we now have is what to do about our long distance love affair."

Sharon's story demonstrates the important role that the female partner has in finding a solution to a potentially devastating sexual problem. Ira's impotence was a difficulty for him in terms of his ego and manhood, yet not one for her. Their openness, and ability to communicate their sexual feelings allowed them to finally reach a mutually satisfying place. No doubt this story would have had a different ending if she was not accepting of him. Because of Sharon's support, there was a need to avoid the sexual aspect of their intimacy.

For many couples, the sexual problem is merely a symptom of other problems in the relationship. A couple lacking a true connection, bonding, and the ability to talk to each other will not be able to handle any difficulties, let alone ones of a sensitive and ego-threatening variety. Couples who have difficulty in expressing their feelings, especially angry ones, may avoid the verbal confrontation by silently withholding in the bedroom. The woman may have problems in becoming sexually stimulated. The man may remain flaccid. Each can be a nonverbal statement that they are not desirous of fulfilling their partner. The solution here may be counseling for the relationship rather than an attempt to "fix" his potency.

> **THE PARTNER'S ROLE**
> *Don't avoid the issue-or him*
> *Support him-tell him that you love and care*
> *Separate sexual potency issues from feelings of love*
> *Be truthful, it doesn't help to save his feelings by saying that intercourse is not important*
> *Don't expect him to be "cured" just because you are communicating*
> *Kiss and hold, but consummation needs to wait*
> *Let him in on your fears of being unloved and sexually unattractive*
> *Seek solutions together*

In a situation where a woman feels that there is a missing ingredient, such as sex or passion in her primary relationship, she may seek it out in another partner. Because she cannot have it all with one man, she finds two men. The woman splits her perception of her mates into two arbitrary categories. One man will fit neatly into one category, the other man into the other category. While one man provides terrific sex, the other provides emotional stability. This can occur when the woman is unable to accept having a relationship with only one man, and so she keeps her

The Men Out There

relationship at a distance. She chooses from the men out there and finds two who can satisfy her specific needs. While we neither condemn nor condone this behavior, we acknowledge the many tales of the other man.

Robin and Tyler had been together for six years, living separately but seeing each other often. On occasion they had lived together. The relationship has suffered many ups and downs. Recently Robin began to see another man. "I never had the kind of fairy tale relationships that some of my friends have. From the time that I was in college, there has always been a disastrous element to my men. I thought that it would be different with Tyler. He was the man who my mother approved of. He would have given me the perfect life. We are the same religion and come from similar backgrounds. He is nice looking and makes a good living. He wants to start a family and we have been together for years. We have tried to make it work. I tried to love him but the sex has never been good.

"I felt like there was something wrong with me. Why couldn't I love this wonderful man? I was the aggressor sexually and he held back. He came too fast and this business of premature ejaculation is very serious. It really destroyed the sex for me. Aside from that, there was no romance in the relationship. I had to set the stage, it never came from him. I

> **OPTIONS AND ALTERNATIVES**
> *Seek information-support groups are a resource*
> *Self-help techniques aid many potency problems*
> *Diagnose whether the problem is physical or psychological*
> *Sex therapy and psychological counseling are effective where there is a psychological origin*
> *A variety of medical options are now available for physical problems: surgery, injections, implants-discover what's right for your partner and you*

> **UNSATISFYING SEX**
>
> *Sex is a barometer for what else is going on*
>
> *If you run to another, your primary relationship is doomed*
>
> *Women need to face that sex is a big part of the picture*
>
> *The answer lies within the relationship*

thought I could teach him but I couldn't. I encouraged him to go to therapy, not for the sex, but in general. He refused. Eventually I started having affairs. I had to get what was missing from the relationship with Tyler. I have met some amazing men and the affairs have made me feel alive.

"Tyler is such a normal guy, he is like a brother to me. He is a very safe man to have in my life. The other guys are on the fringe, and that makes it both more exciting and more dangerous. I do not want to have another Tyler for a lover, but I want another experience, of a completely different order. Eventually I left the relationship with Tyler, gathering strength to do so from the affairs. Recently I have met someone who is better for me. I feel it is a new beginning, a second chance. There is real potential for this to work out. There is sex, romance and caring in one package."

Monica and Ian have been married for three years. Having met when Monica was immersed in an unhappy relationship, she finds the marriage to be particularly gratifying. "I was forty-one when I met Ian and had given up on the idea of having children and a husband. I was content to simply tolerate my long standing relationship and find other avenues of interest. Ian changed everything for me. He was my friend and lover from the start. I admit that we fell into bed immediately and that is not the best way to begin, but it was a success for us. After endless sex there is endless love. We are partners in life and having had the sex first is almost an ironic spin. It has worked in our favor. Had I not met Ian I would not have believed that such a

The Men Out There

> **HOW TO MAKE IT WORK**
> *Time is on your side, use it*
> *Intimacy and passion are important precursors to the sexual act*
> *Make love leisurely, plan ahead*
> *Pressuring him increases the dificulties*
> *Work on your verbal communication in order to communicate physically*
> *Best friends become best mates*
> *When all else fails, seek a professional*

blend was possible. We are so wild about each other physically but we also love to spend time together and to share a life.

"It is a happy situation, after much disappointment and abuse. I was taught that sex did not go with love. I was taught that if there is great passion, the flame will burn out. You cannot expect to be with a man and find a provider and a sexual being in one person. Ian has taught me otherwise. I am now pregnant with our child—a girl. When I became pregnant, I thought that the sex would die down, that Ian would not find me desirable. But it is the opposite. He thinks the pregnancy is a turn on. There is nothing that I do that is not appealing to him. I am very fortunate. I am living proof that sex not only counts but is a big part of the right relationship.

SEX AND LOVE IN ONE

Sex should be emotionally satisfying as well as physically satisfying. Both partners get what they want from the experience. You will not feel lonely or sad. You should feel wanted, loved and cherished. There should be a certain sense of happiness and completion. You will still speak and hold one another afterward. You will look forward to the next interlude.

12

"Two hearts are better than one."
— Bruce Springsteen

THE MAN I LOVE

This time the difference is obvious. You have achieved the capacity for a mature love. You're not sixteen, but forty. You have each weathered the trials and tribulations of life. You and this man are attached in a meaningful way, choosing to be there for each other. You embrace each other's lives and circumstances. The compromises and sacrifices are worth it. This is your odyssey and you have learned what it requires to get you where your heart lies. After many months, perhaps years of searching and experiencing, you are educated enough to appreciate this man when he comes your way. If you have had a preconceived notion of who he will be, and surprisingly he does not exactly fit the bill, you are able to embrace his persona anyway. You are ready to fall in love with the man and not the image of the man. Friendship is a large part of the mix and the loving relationship is authentic. In this union, there is no deliberating, no equivocating. The feelings are genuine and come from the heart. Because there is nourishment, the idea of a commitment is not a threat or something you have to push for, but evolves naturally.

A healthy love relationship is based on companionship, trust, commitment, communication, chemistry, affection. In past decades, relationships were based on financial requirements, and the demands of physical protection. This is not so today. The focus is on nurturing your partner and respecting his uniqueness. *Honoring the man you love and the relationship you share creates a positive situation. Within these boundaries is the potential for a rich and happy life together.*

In order to go forward in a healthy mode, you must stop living in the past or in the future. If you hold onto the past, you will be crippled and unable to appreciate the man you love. You will not be able to recognize him, because your vision is blurred. No two men are going to be alike and their styles will be distinct. It is unhealthy and unwise to make your new partner into your old one. Whatever baggage you each bring to the table, it is significant that you discard it immediately, for both your sakes.

Jocelyn and Daniel were introduced by a mutual friend. They hit it off at once and began to date exclusively within a few weeks time. Jocelyn, at the age of forty-two, had two young children at home. Daniel, at the same age, had one daughter in high school. "For us, it was an instant chemistry. But the feelings fell into place also. Although I had been divorced for several years and had been in several relationships, nothing was

---

TIME SHARED WITH THE MAN YOU LOVE

You do not have to beg for intimacy
There is no game playing
Your desires are sated and so are his
There is a give and take
There are no tugs of power
Space is granted
There are no demands, only solutions

satisfying. My bond to my ex-husband was ongoing because he lived nearby and saw the children frequently. It seemed that his attachment to the kids and to me kept me from forming any real relationships with any other men. I was quite hurt and my ego was destroyed when he asked me for a divorce. When we became divorced, we still hadn't severed things completely. I knew that getting back with him was out of the question, but whenever I saw him or whenever we made plans over the telephone, I felt the tug.

"I had to come to realize that it was alright to still have feelings about my ex-husband. Those feelings were not going to go away. Instead of deciding to wait and see if these feelings would dissipate, I realized I had to move on with my life. I learned I could care for someone new without giving up the feelings for my ex-husband. We had a long history together. The children and all of the good memories won't disappear. The insight I gleaned came from meeting Daniel and realizing I could care about him in an entirely different way. I did not have to let go of what had been with my ex-husband in order to love Daniel. There are similarities and differences between these men. Although I miss aspects of the relationship with my ex-husband, I know that the relationship ultimately could not work out. And I treasure the positive aspects of my new relationship with Daniel."

REGAINING FAITH IN LOVE

When a relationship ends, women often feel they will not be able to love again. The injury has been so acute that the healing process is not complete. Meeting a new mate can actually expedite things, but only if you are willing to allow yourself to heal. Rather than first looking outward, for a new relationship as the impetus for feeling better, it is wise to look inward. Thus the faith is rejuvenated.

The Men Out There

After a long standing relationship or marriage has come to an end, it is not easy to be on your own again. The language of the old relationship, regardless of its lack of success, haunts you. You are with a new partner, but the shadow of the old and your shared ways linger. As in Woody Allen's film, *Annie Hall*, there is the need to recapture a lost past. He and Diane Keaton's character are about to boil live lobsters when the lobsters go scurrying across the kitchen floor. They both become hysterical and share the moment. Once he and Keaton's character are no longer united, he attempts to repeat the scene with another woman and it fails. We cannot go back, but can honor a relationship based on its own essence. It is dangerous when we attempt to make the new relationship into something else, something identical to what we once had.

The loving relationship that grew between Shelley and Matt was unexpected. Shelley, the mother of a small girl, had been in an unhappy marriage for seven years. Yet when she separated she felt thrown to the wolves. Matt had been married briefly to his college girlfriend and had no children. "We met at a business dinner and were instantly attracted. I was quite gun shy after a lonely marriage and Matt was on the prowl. We began a physical relationship almost at once. What was amazing was that the sex was so important from the start. While the sex was incredible, it wasn't only about sex. This was about love and caring. I could not believe that there was a man who could make me feel good.

"I had been so disappointed in my marriage. The very idea of spending a Saturday with a man was alien to me, I had always run away from my husband, figuratively speaking. We had never spent time together on a weekend unless it involved other couples. Now I was with someone who wanted to be with me and I with him. He was so kind to my son, I could not believe it. Having a man in the wings definitely gave me the courage to be okay about becoming divorced. I don't know if I could have done it without Matt's love and protection. I ended up being divorced and remarried within a few months time. I know that what I felt for my first husband cannot be compared to what I feel for Matt. Today, ten years later, my ex-husband and I are close friends but as husband and wife it was empty. What remains after a divorce is the loss of hope and success. I was fortunate to be given the opportunity to try again."

HE WILL APPEAR UNEXPECTEDLY

The way to meet the man you love cannot be planned. He is around the corner, and waiting for you. You must live your life in the meantime, and not be in constant search. Once he appears, energy, effort, and time will make it happen.

In a true love relationship, friendship starts it off and spins it into orbit. Friendship is a significant aspect of the relationship and cannot be diminished. If you are not friends first, if you do not like one another, the love cannot survive. When a man is truly enamored of you, he pays you great attention. He will call simply to hear your voice, he will introduce you to his family and to his friends. He will respect your work and your interests, he will come to your home to pick you up. This man who you love will not ask you to leave his bed when the sex is finished, but will want you beside him in the morning. He will tell you how he feels, and he will be totally sincere. If he is a man who cannot express himself, he will show you by his actions.

After being single for four years, Alynne, forty-one, met Malcolm, thirty-nine, at a Halloween party. He had never been married, and was quite ready to take the journey. "I don't think that we would ever have sought each other out based on a resume. It was the face to face meeting, without any discomfort like on a blind date, that made things possible. While I do not know love at first sight for a fact, I had this feeling when I met Malcolm. I knew he and I had something, some kind of connection. We were engaged within eight weeks. People who knew us went crazy, they thought it was too soon and remarked that we didn't really know each other. They all warned us that it couldn't last. But I had dated a lot and I felt and saw the difference.

"There were logistics to work out because we lived eighty miles from each other and we both had jobs in our home towns. In the end, Malcolm was able to relocate. I insisted that I give up my apartment and that we start fresh. He agreed. So we bought a place that is all ours. When I think of the other men who I carefully considered for a lifelong partner, I know that I was deluding myself. I was trying to make it fit. Some were handsomer than Malcolm, and some were more successful, but he is the one for me. We do not give each other a difficult time, instead we try to anticipate what would make each other happy. He is generous and kind to me. These are the things that matter. Especially when it is a second chance and the second half of life. We have spoken of having a family together. I feel a biological clock ticking, but I also feel so confident that whatever happens, it is right for us."

THERE ARE NO MYTHS

Fantasies are not necessary with the man you love. You are able to recognize your needs and that they are met. You listen to yourself and are not influenced by anyone else. He becomes your priority because it is what you choose, it is all about you and him. The love is kept going by communication and realistic expectations. You suit each other's needs and can be supportive. In a shared life, you grow together. There is equality and the ability to confront issues when they arise.

_____ Susan R. Shapiro and Michele Kasson, Ph.D.

Many women who end up with the man they love do not speak of romance as much as they speak of understanding and compassion. In this chapter, there is no description of lust and longing, but of comfort and trust. A continual energy is poured into the relationship and the dividend is apparent. There is no complacency but a tremendous appreciation of one another. The love is renewed on a daily basis, and stability rules the day. Although we realize from experience that love is never enough, we tend to hold onto the myth which contradicts this fact. Regardless of the depth of love in a relationship, if there is too much disparity in background or values or goals, it will not prevail.

Once burned, twice shy, each of us has had an entanglement which has left us hurt and with high walls. In literature and the movies we have witnessed successful and unsuccessful bonding with the man one loves. In the heart wrenching film, *The Way We Were*, Streisand's and Redford's characters are ill fated from the start. Despite their love for one another, there is no common ground to hold the marriage together and it dissolves, leaving a trail of heartache. When they run into each other at the end of the movie, each with a new mate, it is evident that despite their differences, the old love has not died. On a happier note, the movie *Indecent Proposal* offers the couple a wake up call. Demi Moore's character is

> **WHEN LOVE FITS, IT LASTS**
> *There must be shared values*
> *Compatibility is required*
> *There is responsibility to the other*
> *There is mutual respect*
> *There is honesty and trust*
> *You are available to one another*
> *True love evokes inner strength—you become a better person*
> *You are best friends*
> *There is chemistry*
> *There is commitment, a certain kind of tenacity*
> *There is acceptance*

shocked when Robert Redford's character offers to pay one million dollars to sleep with her, and Woody Harrelson, who plays her husband, agrees to accept it. After much upset to their lives, the newlyweds are reunited, with a heightened sense of appreciation for each other.

In the case of Amy and the man she loves, it has been a rocky road. Divorced with two children, Amy moved back to her hometown and rediscovered Herman, a man she had dated in high school over twenty years ago. "I had really liked him and would have pursued the relationship after high school, but we went our different ways and ended up in colleges in different parts of the country. I later heard that he was married, but by then I already had a child and was pregnant with my second. Still I thought of him on many days when I was alone with my babies. We lost touch and then I heard about a year ago that he had left his marriage and was moving back home. He had been living on the east coast all these years and I'd been in Northern California. Back home, we met for dinner and it was as if we'd never missed a beat. Really and truly, it's as if we are meant to be together. We've grown older but we have not changed, we are basically the same but seasoned by life. Being together today is like a great gift. He is one of those people who needs to be remarried. He wants to have a quiet, uncomplicated life. The single scene is not for him. I know who the men are out there and I did not want them. Then I saw Herman again and it all fell into place."

INDEPENDENT LOVE

It is important for you to remain independent when you are with the man you love. If you lose yourself, the relationship will fail. You must nurture each other while remaining two separate entities.

_____ Susan R. Shapiro and Michele Kasson, Ph.D.

Our realistic expectations of love have been influenced by the media, networks, and film industry. We are taught that committed love lasts through thick and thin. Juxtaposed with this myth are numerous examples of people who walk because they do not have what it takes to remain. No wonder we are so confused, we are taught two different scenarios, encouraged to choose as best we can.

The man you love will take strides to satisfy you sexually. Your pleasures are his and there is a fusion which takes place during the lovemaking that is healthy and healing in nature. Honest sex is found in a loving relationship—there is a blending of body and soul.

While some women have described the sex with the man they love as less satisfying and exciting than with a man they lusted after, they are able to recognize the nature of sex with the former. Sex is not always a motivating force in a loving relationship, or the driving energy, but it has to be a component, a part of the mix of friendship, and the extraordinary feelings of being connected to this partner.

Antonia's lover is her companion and grants her freedom. After several years of dating without finding anyone to commit to, she is thrilled, but hesitant to give herself over to Fred. "We share a mutual trust and we believe in each other. Men and women are different—that I've learned the hard way. If a man tells me that I'm too good for him, I know now to believe him. If he tells me that he feels we are right for each other, I know that I can believe that too. I now understand what can and cannot work in a relationship. Fred is in my corner, and is there to take care of me, and I take care of him too. In terms of sex, it is wonderful. Intellectually it is rewarding too, but I know that my girlfriends can provide me with intellectual stimulation. I'm very independent but a partner fits into my life. It is how society has conditioned me, and most adults, not only women. With Fred, there is a completeness, a closing of the circle. I have finally found the right partner."

To presume to know anything about another couple is naive and unfair, for in most cases, the two players themselves are baffled by the interchange. There are famous couples who have absolutely struck a deal, such as Hugh Grant and Elisabeth Hurley, Miss Piggy and Kermit, Bill and Hillary Clinton. Yet there is some connection which creates the glue, which keeps them together and committed to each other. Whether they meet the requirements that we recommend or not is another story. The questions to ask yourself as you embark on a journey with the man you love are the following:

IS THIS THE MAN I LOVE?

Has he met enough women or is he still on a dating frenzy?
Is he capable of accepting you?
Does he want a partner?
Is he emotionally stable?
Is he simply infatuated?
Is he smothering or encouraging?
Is the timing right for him?

The important discussions should not be hedged. If your partner is against having babies and you are yearning for one, it needs to be addressed. If you make more money than he or vice versa, the expectations should be established early on. How the finances will affect the structure of the relationship ought to be set at the start. The demands of each career need to be understood—disparate careers can take their toll. Real life issues and reactions to them are a part of daily life—his reactions must be compatible with yours.

Susan R. Shapiro and Michele Kasson, Ph.D.

> **LIVING IN THE PRESENT**
>
> Take each day as it comes
>
> Do not make plans that are far in the future
>
> Spend time together when it is convenient
>
> Do not bombard each other with dates and plans
>
> Begin as friends
>
> Don't fantasize about what your love will become

After several unhappy relationships, Mary found that meeting Neil at a party was an unexpected surprise. "If my friend had not coaxed me along, I would never have met Neil. He was also there alone, and we found each other immediately. We have been dating ever since. We are moving slowly but seriously into a committed relationship. It is as if neither of us can recall anyone else in our lives. Everything we do is new. Neil is eight years younger than I am, which is something I have never done before, and our backgrounds are very different. He comes from an intellectual family and teaches at a university nearby. I'm from a working class background. I am an addiction counselor which is a big deal in my family.

"There is great chemistry in the relationship and he is also gentle, talkative, and a good listener. We love to do the same things, listen to music, eat the same foods. It all feels very familiar and safe.

"At this stage in my life I do not plan to marry again. I am forty-two and I already have two children. I expect nothing from Neil except a good weekend. I do not mind that I am older than he is, I do not mind the days we spend apart. I am very comfortable in this relationship. There are no doubts. He is delightful to be with, and is showing me what a mature relationship is all about."

In a truly successful love relationship, there is a caring that moves one through the stages of romantic love to an emotional depth. In the beginning stages, romance happens quickly and there is a spark and chemistry, followed by a great urge to be with one another physically and emotionally. We have our fantasies and illusions of what the love will be and how terrific and fabulous our lives will be once we have our ideal partner. *The passion is at its peak but when it wanes, there must be more to hold it together than the illusive quality of romance. This needs to be replaced with an altruistic devotion that is the base of a loving relationship. In this case, there is real give and take and an approach to life that is shared and valued. With our partner, and the word partner is chosen carefully for these purposes, there is an unselfish quality which gives substance and meaning to one's life.*

Kristen, who was born in Sweden and came to the States to attend college, has never been married. At the age of thirty-five, she met Tony, and has spent the past nine months with him, living together in a small town in rural Vermont. "Neither of us belong here, which is probably why we found each other. He is a chef at a restaurant and I am working at a small hotel, as the manager. My family strongly objected to Tony at the beginning because of our different backgrounds. I think that an American would be acceptable, but not an Italian American. Then something happened that made my family change their mind. About five months ago, I became very ill with cancer and Tony has been phenomenal. I have been in treatment and he has stayed by my side. I'm in chemo and so I've lost my hair. He tells me that am still beautiful and that he loves me. If he hasn't left by now, I suspect that he never will. I have grown to love him more and more because of his feelings for me and because of his ability to show his love. He is my best friend — it is beyond my wildest dreams. He takes care of me on the days when I'm not feeling well and we have great times together on the days when I feel well. I believe that his love can heal me. Since my family has seen the love that

_____ Susan R. Shapiro and Michele Kasson, Ph.D.

Tony gives to me, they have changed their minds. He is absolutely welcome anytime."

BEST FRIENDS

You can anticipate each other's needs and wishes. There is intimacy and an empathy that is both verbal and non-verbal communication. Loyalty and devotion are present without demand. The commitment comes from the caring and not from expectations or external forces. It is renewed on a daily basis. Best friends understand that the ordinary is fine and the extraordinary is unnecessary, it is only the ribbon on the package.

Grace and Raphael have been together for one year. Both were previously married, and scarred by the experience. "Raphael and I have a great deal of respect for each other. That's the bottom line. I was very hurt in my marriage, and although I have dated and had relationships with other men since my marriage, I was always too fearful to give my heart. My friends were aware of my feelings for Raphael before I was because of how I talked about him. Since the beginning he has been steadfast and dependable. He knows that I am like a frightened bird, ready to take flight at any sudden move, so rather than push me, he lets me lean on his solidity. He doesn't have to tell me that he loves me because it is so obvious by how he treats me. Our daily living makes it difficult for us to be together, or to share as much down time together as we would want. Still, I am relaxed, knowing that emotionally he is there with me. Sure, we have had our ups and downs, but we have faith that we can get through the tough times because we work at communicating. It's hard to do, and neither of us had been very good at it in our marriages. Both of us are committed to making it work out. When I first got divorced, I only wanted to quickly remarry so that

I would not be single. Now I am in no rush to marry, just content to spend time with the man I love."

FORGIVENESS AND TENDERNESS

The man you love requires honesty and respect. In return, he honors the relationship and is able to feel the spiritual bond. You are not rigid with one another but kind and understanding. There is no power play but a mutual give and take. You no longer look at other men because the one you love is standing before you.

Alexis and Martin, both thirty-eight, had known one another for nine months before they became lovers. The relationship had time periods when they did not speak with one another, so that Alexis believed that Martin was not interested in her romantically. "I spent more time with Martin having dinner and talking about our lives without being friends or lovers. It was actually a very strange situation. I found him physically attractive and very kind. I thought he was one of the nicest men I had ever met. But in a society where looks are accentuated, I found myself suspicious of Martin's ability to be a good guy. He showed me the way by simply being himself. He never hurt me and it was so refreshing, so unique to any man I've ever known. By the time that we began to sleep together, it just felt like it was right. We have the same goals, and yet none of it is discussed, but understood.

"I had been so hurt in my marriage and so hurt in a

> **SURRENDERING YOUR LOVE**
>
> - When you love someone, you give to get
> - Both the ups and downs are accepted
> - There is a blending of souls and a distinction of souls
> - Love at first sight grows into friendship and common goals
> - There is compromise and communication

relationship. I never expected to meet anyone who would make me happy. I began to think that dating was fine, and was all that I could handle. I'm very busy as an attorney, and the work that Martin does keeps him busy too—he's a physician. With our schedules being what they are, we often have work over the weekends.

> **WHAT TO DO TO MAKE IT RIGHT**
>
> Don't let the past into the present relationship
>
> Give it time and energy
>
> Do not be critical, but do not overlook his faults either
>
> Be open minded and ready for love—experience the joy of each new day with your new man
>
> Don't allow your fears to be the deciding factor
>
> Work at communication-listening and responding to each others needs

We do not mind working together, at my place. We are very compatible that way. And I simply take it one day at a time. We do not speak of the future or of having children. But the time that we share feels good and real to me. That is all that I can ask for. And when I see him walking down the street, I'm so happy that he's coming toward me, that we are about to go out together somewhere, anywhere—at all. He shows me courtesy and decency. I am thrilled to be with him."

THERE IS NO PERFECT MAN

In search of the man you love, one must remember that illusion is dangerous and that it is a matter of sifting through the good and bad in anyone. To idealize a mate is to lose the potential for a true loving relationship. The trick is to choose wisely, find the man who suits your needs and does not harp on the negative. It takes time to fall in love, and to discard the ghosts of the past. In mid-life we come to relationships with baggage and battle scars. It is only with confidence and faith that one goes forward to begin again.

Afterword

Women of any age have been taught to believe that a loving partner will make all the difference in their lives. Despite their autonomy and force, there is the underlying fear of facing the future alone. The media and the society at large influence the lives that women choose, and dictate what we can and cannot have. The valuable lesson learned is that it is only when a woman feels absolutely good about herself and can be alone that she does not have to be alone. It is only when we are strong and fearless that we become attractive to any and every man out there. At this point she does not require a relationship with the first man who comes into her life. She is able to put herself on the line, risk it all, in order to obtain the relationship she desires. It is then that the patterns of the past are shed.

In our attempt to research the men out there and the women who know them, we were drawn into an unexpected and unknown universe. In listening to hundreds of stories, a common theme for women became apparent, that is the desire to find a soulful, loving partner, and to achieve a prosperous relationship. Whether women have been married or in long standing unions, there is the expectation that they will at last come to some conclusion with a significant other. They have matured to a point

The Men Out There

where they are hopefully able to realize what is positive for them and what is not. What we have gleaned from the real life tales are mixed reviews of the men out there. Whatever the outcome, it is these revelations which have guided us.

Recent generations have suffered much disappointment in love. The long standing marriage of fifty years ago that our parents have enjoyed or endured is not to be anticipated. The norm today is to be divorced and perhaps remarried or with a lover for an extended period of time. The commitment and expectation of the past is nonexistent in today's world. It has been replaced by a population of bruised men and women, in dire search of a second chance.

In *The Men Out There* the categories of men we have created were based on women's anonymous stories which presented recurring themes. Because both men and women are multidimensional, these types were constructed as a way to teach us about specific men. *The definitions of men which we have provided offer women the opportunity to recognize their mate. For men it is an opportunity to rediscover themselves.* While the structure may appear to be rigid, it is not. Very often a tendency in one chapter crosses over to another chapter. In other words, a narcissist who makes a great deal of money can also be a money and power man. The instant family man may have been a workaholic before he reached the point of settling down and reorganizing his energies. The man addicted to alcohol and or drugs may also have a penchant for gambling and women. The married man may also be a workaholic. We have discovered that within each type of man presented are characteristics of other types of men. The categories were not written in stone but exemplify notable traits of the men out there.

When we first began to write this book, we intended it to be read by women everywhere, as an aid in educating

_____ Susan R. Shapiro and Michele Kasson, Ph.D.

themselves about failed or flourishing relationships. By the time that we had completed it, we realized that *The Men Out There* is not written only for women but for men as well. *Any man out there can gain insight into his own behavior by leafing through these pages.* What the reader learns is that men and women come to the same place in distinct ways. Often a woman feels that a man is absent in a relationship, while the man feels that the woman engulfs him. Yet within these interpretations, there is room to evolve and to attend to one another's needs.

What we have heard repeatedly is that a woman's search for the "right" man has earned her the ability to reject the "wrong" man. However, when two people fall in love, the basis for this mutual caring is that they suit each other. If you are not feeling happy or deriving pleasure from a relationship, then your requirements are not being met. Having read the book, a woman who finds herself in this place is advised to face the facts and to move on. *The Men Out There* provides this tool, a method of recognizing what is missing from the relationship or what enhances a relationship. When things are working in a positive manner, our book affirms this. The reader is able to identify with the patterns.

We have learned through this exploration that men's styles vary by degrees. If a style is exaggerated in a specific category and a man's reaction to his partner is very strong, a woman has a choice. Either she can make the effort to keep it going or she can move on because she is not satisfied. While specific scenarios are untenable, others are possibilities, with work, effort, and constancy. One must decide if it is worth it. When a relationship works, it is because both partners are willing to give and take, to stablilize and support one another. *In a loving relationship, the initial infatuation turns to admiration and respect.* What is necessary is an established comfort level that shoulders all other aspects of the bond: sex, romance, trust, commitment, the baggage of children, elderly parents, the real fabric of everyday living.

The men out there have weathered difficult times. The historical role of man has been altered. The hunter/warrior is no longer required. His masculinity, previously defined as such, gave him clarity and lack of turmoil. In the current society, his role is not as defined. Thus he seeks ways to define his masculinity. It is his confusion about his place in the world that makes him uneasy in his role with women. This may not be true of every man. There are definitely those who are comfortable with themselves. This man knows his masculinity yet is able to be a sensitive mate. *The key recognition is that there is no ideal man. There is a man who has more qualities that you appreciate and less of those that you disdain. It is this understanding that enables us to have a lasting relationship.*